P9-CME-067

PRINCESS Diana

Her Life Story
1961–1997

An Unauthorized Biography
By Richard Buskin

PUBLICATIONS INTERNATIONAL, LTD.

All rights reserved under International and Pan American copyright conventions. Copyright © 1997 Publications International, Ltd. All rights reserved. This book may not be reproduced or quoted in whole or in part by any means whatsoever without written permission from Louis Weber, C.E.O. of Publications International, Ltd., 7373 North Cicero Avenue, Lincolnwood, Illinois 60646. Permission is never granted for commercial purposes. Printed in U.S.A.

Richard Buskin is a British journalist who has conducted interviews and written articles for a wide variety of publications, including the *Observer Magazine, Paris Match,* the *New York Post,* and the *Sydney Morning Herald.* His previous books include the biography *John Lennon: His Life and Legend* and *The Films of Marilyn Monroe,* as well as career retrospectives on Elvis Presley and the Beatles.

Special acknowledgments to the following people for their assistance: Sue Eardley, for her patience and skill in carrying out research and conducting interviews; Lowri Turner, Margaret Holder, Kathy Iuliucci, Allen J. Wiener, Zelda Westmeads, and Dr. Dorothy Rowe, for their information and insight with regard to the complex life of the Princess of Wales; and Raymonde Buskin, for her invaluable editorial assistance.

Contents

I never know where a lens is going to be," the Princess of Wales claimed in a 1995 TV interview. "On a normal day I'll be followed by four cars. On a normal day I'll come back to my car and find six freelance photographers jumping around me."

Diana could hardly have realized that the photographers and their cameras would soon pursue her to her death. Naturally the lenses would be on hand one day to capture the aftermath of her demise, whenever that might be. But not at the moment of her death. That, at least, would be a moment of privacy. . . .

Unfortunately, not as things turned out. Princess Diana's death, the result of an automobile accident in Paris during the early hours of a late-Summer morning in 1997, produced a horror-story ending to what had once been everyone's favorite fairy tale. It was the story of a poor little rich girl from a broken home who grew up to marry a prince.

With untold riches at her fingertips and an adoring nation virtually eating out of her hand, the glamorous Princess effortlessly charmed the masses in a manner and on a scale that Britain's royal family had rarely, if ever, achieved. Around the world, people were in awe of Diana's style, her grace, her demeanor, and

Diana waves a practiced "hello" to her people.

her immensely affable persona. Yet, as time went on and chinks began to appear in the presumably blissful marriage, it became clear that among the very few people Diana couldn't enchant were her husband and her in-laws.

Theirs was not a match made in heaven. What it did produce, however, in addition to "the heir and the spare" to the throne, was a complete turnaround in how the general public would ever after perceive the royals. A welcome breath of fresh air in what has long been regarded as an extremely stuffy environment, Diana didn't actually modernize "the firm" (as the Queen and those around her refer to themselves), but she did at least provide people with considerable hope that the Windsors would somehow be dragged into the twenty-first century, instead of forever languishing as relics of a bygone era.

In the meantime, Diana's most enduring contribution on the royal front has been to highlight how drastically the family's image is in need of an overhaul. In fact, her life and now her death, have played a large part in calling the entire future of Britain's monarchy into question.

Although some of what she did during her later years didn't always meet with universal approval, Di was, for all intents and purposes, a Princess of (and for) the people. That is, a jet-set princess who lived out people's far-flung

Diana brought an heir, and a breath of fresh air to the royal Windsors.

fantasies while always appearing to care for those in need. Her championing of causes such as the fight against AIDS, and the Red Cross campaign to ban land mines, won her worldwide respect. Her evident kindness also garnered an affection that was best symbolized by the mass outpouring of grief in the days following her death.

Princess Diana passed away at the premature age of 36, and she is destined to become an icon, forever young and forever surrounded by controversy. Diana's was an action-packed existence, cramming into those 36 years events that would normally comprise several lifetimes. It was a life of the most fantastic highs and miserable lows, of pride and embarrassment, achievement and loss, and happiness as well as tragedy. Often thwarted in her attempts to find true love in a one-on-one relationship, she was nevertheless adored by millions.

Diana was a woman of notable contradictions who made her fair share of bad decisions, not the least of which involved the men with whom she chose to have intimate relationships. Her clear-cut desire to maintain a high profile while coveting some much-needed privacy also comes to mind. Indeed, after spending nearly 17 years in the full glare of the media spotlight, Diana never seemed to fully grasp that when she used the press for her own ends, she was doing so on their terms.

Still, it was her shortcomings, as well as an emotional fragility, that pushed her beyond depression into several suicide attempts. All of which made Diana all the more human in the eyes of the public. This, of course, was especially true when contrasting her obvious warmth with the well-mannered but often implacable stoicism of her regal associates. When Diana greeted her children after spending some time away she did so with hugs and kisses. Who, on the other hand, could forget the image of the Queen returning to England after a six-month tour overseas, and reacquainting herself with eight-year-old Charles by way of a formal handshake?

Protocol and tradition are what the royal family is largely about; of remaining "class-less" in an extremely class-conscious society, and maintaining a status quo that keeps them at the top of the social pecking order while pursuing a way of life that places them in a sort of time-warp. Having entered this world from left-field, Diana chose to buck the system and regain her freedom. But she did so at a price, and for the privilege of traveling without royal bodyguards she eventually paid with her life.

This is a story with an average beginning, a happy middle, and a tragic ending. From the birth of Lady Diana Frances Spencer to the death of the Princess of Wales, it encompasses the good and the bad, and leaves us not only with a life and potential unfulfilled, but also the legacy of a young woman who touched people's hearts, captured their imagination, and changed the course of history.

"Nothing gives me more pleasure now than being able to love and help those in our society who are vulnerable," Diana told *Vanity Fair* in an interview conducted just a few months before her death. "If I can contribute a little something, then I am more than content."

In truth, considering what she gave of herself and the effect that she had on the world, Diana should now be overjoyed.

CHAPTER 1

DIANA'S STORY: PRIVATE ANGUISH, PUBLIC TRAUMA

When 700 million people in 74 countries around the world tuned in their television sets on Wednesday, July 29, 1981, they knew what they were looking for. They wanted to see Lady Diana Spencer step down from a glass coach in front of St. Paul's Cathedral in London. They wanted to see the fabulous gown in which she was about to wed Charles, Prince of Wales. And more than anything else, the 700 million people wanted to witness the fulfillment of the ultimate fantasy: the marriage of a beautiful young girl to a dashing prince in his fairy-tale kingdom. They looked toward the promise of life lived happily ever after. It was a marriage that brought untold riches and the promised love of the new

Princess Diana was the most popular member of Britain's royal family.

princess's people. It was a grand moment, and in homes across the globe, 700 million viewers could not take their eyes off the splendid sight.

The girl did marry her prince, and she did get to live in palatial splendor amid an opulent lifestyle. And she had the love of her adoring public. Yet the rest of the fairy tale eluded Diana. It remains only the stuff of dreams, romantic novels, and old-fashioned Hollywood movies. For the television viewers could not have known that behind the cultured looks and the shy smile there was a naive, confused 20-year-old, about to enter a loveless marriage, to suffer the consequences of a match made anywhere but in heaven. Aspiring to the dream is one thing, but living it was quite another, and this was a lesson that Diana, the young aristocrat from a broken home, started to learn almost before her marriage began.

The eventual coming to terms with this truth, however, was a long and painful process. And while the Princess of Wales publicly tried to exude an air of dignified serenity, in private she was pushed to the edge of despair, and, on more than one occasion, she almost plummeted over the precipice.

Despite all this, during that time Diana blossomed from a charming, sweet girl, into a highly attractive, self-assured, and gracious woman. At once a loving mother and princess, she attended to a considerable list of royal duties with the same degree of care and dedication as she provided her own two boys. Her most striking physical features were her height—almost six feet tall in heels—her beautiful blonde hair, and crystal blue eyes. According to those who were closest to her, Diana was warm and endearing, with a sharp sense of humor that was often camouflaged by her apparent unimposing manner.

Diana could also be fiery, bullish, incredibly stubborn, and unreasonably demanding in her expectations of those around her. She was not unaware of the resentment that her glamourous image and sometimes flirtatious gestures could inspire in other women. She wanted to be loved, but had little time for those who chose not to admire her.

All this, of course, could have been the result of insecurity stemming from a troubled childhood in which she unjustifiably took upon herself part of the blame for her parents' divorce. It could also be attributed to the fact that Diana married a man to whom she was once wholly dedicated, but who reciprocated little in terms of either warmth or attention.

Either way, one thing was certain: In her own inimitably sweet way, Diana gave the British monarchy a jolt. This was not all bad. Diana's manner and point of view opened the eyes of a country that was steeped in Victoriana—the mode of an earlier age when

The royal family presented a united front at the
50th Anniversary of the Battle of Britain.

Britain still ruled the waves and much of the
world; when the word of British men was law
and the place of proper British women was in
the home. The Victorian era valued appearance
above everything else. If there was philandering
or other scandal in high places, it was discreetly
ignored or hushed up.

The present royal family wanted very much
to continue this proper tradition, despite the fact
that past members of the family had not always
behaved in the accepted manner. Edward VII,
for example, successor and son to Queen
Victoria, happily indulged himself in
extramarital affairs. But royal carryings-on of

this sort were conveniently ignored and royal life continued in the grand, familiar fashion. This method of dealing with royal indiscretion worked acceptably until the 1930s, when Edward VIII threw an enormous wrench into the royal works by opting for abdication in order to experience married life with the commoner (and two-time divorcée), Wallis Simpson.

Somewhat more recently, Princess Margaret provided the royal family with embarrassment and the public with plenty of juicy gossip via her romances with Peter Townsend and Roddy Lewellyn, and her rather short-lived marriage to Tony Armstrong-Jones (later made the Earl of Snowdon).

Over the years, such irregularities have made slight chinks in the royal armor, but they have been sufficiently spaced apart to cause little damage to the monarchy's overall image. This has not been the case in recent times, however, as one royal disaster followed another in such quick succession that the family felt itself reeling under the weight of increasingly adverse and unsympathetic public opinion.

Yet all this came at the end of a halcyon period during the early to mid-eighties when royal popularity was at one of its all-time highs. This was due in no small part to Diana, for her arrival on the scene was like a breath of fresh air pumping new life into the monarchy, revamping its traditionally stuffy image, and changing the public perspective. Suddenly, here was someone whose appearance and whole demeanor gave added depth to the term "royal glamour"—a sweet-faced debutante, who looked equally at ease garbed in traditional costume or modeling the creations of Britain's top fashion designers as she was sporting a baseball cap, T-shirt, and jeans. She was outwardly reserved while retaining youthful vivacity, adding up to the ideal package: a modern-day princess with the style and charisma to capture the imagination of the press and the hearts of the people. The flip side to this coin, however, was that while the glamourous image was called for and expected to a point, it could have a detrimental effect when it was promoted excessively.

Queen Elizabeth II, one of the wealthiest people in the world, has the British public still largely prepared to financially support her closest relatives through the tax system. But in return, the royal family is to represent the British nation at home and abroad, as well as to provide welcome escapism in a frequently cold and cruel world.

On the other hand, especially during periods of economic recession, the British taxpayers are less willing to subsidize a lifestyle more attuned to Beverly Hills than Buckingham Palace. Royal glamour is one thing, but

Hollywood it is not. When lavish amounts of money were apparently being spent on clothes, makeup, and glitzy vacations, and, worse still, the national figureheads behaved in less than royal fashion, tongues began to wag, grievances were aired, and headlines glared. Diana was not the sole culprit in this regard, and not necessarily the worst, either. Still memories are long and people were not apt to forget the time Diana and Sarah Ferguson prodded a friend in the behind with umbrellas at Ascot. Nor the time the two women tried to trip each other up the ski slopes of Klosters. This sort of behavior is amusing and even refreshing, but does not exactly conform to the royal code of conduct. And it was certainly not the way for Diana to gain the approval of her royal mother in-law.

In a class-conscious society, the British monarchy has always strived to remain class-less—above the conventional system. Yet these sorts of antics put the royal family members in severe danger of being portrayed (or worse yet, perceived) as people with more money than brains, or, to fall back on a popular British tabloid phrase, "a bunch of upper-class twits." Perhaps more than ever before, the Queen had her work cut out for her when trying to pull the young perpetrators back in line. It sometimes seemed as though she were fighting an uphill battle.

Yet, through all of that, Diana managed to hang on to her absolute status as the favorite royal. A caring soul, she worked tirelessly for a very long list of charitable causes. Among them were Dr. Barnardo's (Britain's largest child-care institution), the Child Accident Prevention Trust, the housing-related Guinness Trust, and Help the Aged. She was also involved with many health-connected projects relating to drug rehabilitation, deafness, blindness, lung disease, cancer, meningitis, spinal research, Parkinson's disease, leprosy, and AIDS. All of this work deservedly gained her the love and admiration of millions of people around the world.

Furthermore, she was not content in the role of president or patron of these many and varied organizations or to simply act as a figurehead. She went out of her way to promote each cause, to help raise the much-needed funds, and to provide support where she could for those who were ill or for those put in charge of caring for them. Just the simple act of shaking ungloved hands with patients at a London hospital's AIDS unit sent a clear message around the globe, helping to dispel the widespread prejudice and ignorance attached to this horrible disease.

The importance and effect of such work should not be underestimated, and this aspect alone helped justify Diana's lofty position. It also provided people with the perfect reason for liking her. She was seen as generous and kind,

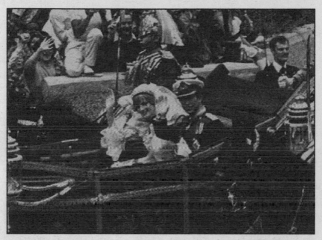

Who would have thought that this marriage would not have a fairy-tale ending?

earning her keep, and therefore worthy of everyone's affection. Everyone, that is, except her husband, a supreme irony in light of the fact that it was his attention and approval that she craved the most in the early days of their marriage.

What follows is a story of romance, heartache, loneliness, fabulous recognition, and unfulfilled dreams. It is the tale of a poor little rich girl who was forced to grow up quickly and to reassess her values in life. The story is worthy of the longest running soap opera, and it is a story that ends far too soon.

CHAPTER 2

SCOOP: THE DREAM BECAME A NIGHTMARE

The royal marriage, which had been launched with such high hopes just 11 months earlier, was already on the rocks by the time the couple's firstborn child, Prince William, entered the world on June 21, 1982, ten days short of Diana's 21st birthday.

It took little time for the Princess to realize that she was less than happy with many aspects of the lifestyle she had married into. She may have come from a solidly aristocratic background, but this was an altogether different world of royal protocol and high-profile public exposure. She felt ill at ease carrying out her scheduled duties—a never-ending cycle of meeting people, shaking hands, and giving speeches—made especially difficult when her every word and movement were captured by the

Princess Diana's second pregnancy was a very emotionally trying time for her.

world's television cameras and press photographers.

Worse still, all lines of communication with her new husband were rapidly breaking down. Whenever Diana expressed to him the way she felt, Charles appeared to brush her feelings aside, while reminding her of their considerable responsibilities. At the same time, no amount of persuading by the future king or the circle of royal advisers seemed to convince the Princess to take her role more seriously. Aware that her popularity with the masses had already been firmly established, she saw no need to apply herself further in any way. She naively thought that if anyone was going to alter their habits it would have to be those around her. The problem was that while her main priority was to cement the family unit, her spouse's was in pursuing the traditional pastimes and duties of the Prince of Wales, and nothing was going to change that.

Diana was feeling increasingly isolated, and matters were not made any easier by the inescapable fact that on an intellectual level, husband and wife were obviously worlds apart. He enjoyed classical music and serious drama, while she preferred pop music and TV soaps; he enjoyed reading serious literature, she was only interested in romantic novels and fashion magazines. He enjoyed fox hunting and grouse shooting. She had an aversion to blood sports, even though her own background had been steeped in this kind of social activity. Charles felt best suited to life in the country, while Diana was more comfortable staying in town; his idea of the perfect vacation was to go skiing in Switzerland, hers was to sit by a swimming pool and soak up the sun. Clearly, they were separated by more than just 12 years in age.

As Charles began to lose more and more interest in Diana, she read this as a lack of love on his part, without apparently considering that perhaps a gesture of her own love would be to try and become attuned to his tastes and desires. Charles, too, could have been more flexible, but he needed intellectual as well as emotional fulfillment, and without it there was a complete breakdown on both sides. In short, it was stubbornness as much as incompatibility that helped erode the marriage, since neither one seemed at all interested in adhering to the rules of give-and-take. They evidently did not do enough homework on each other before the wedding.

"He knew when he was marrying her that she had had insufficient education at the kind of schools where girls were not intended to have careers," asserts Margaret Holder, a leading royal observer, and contributor to books and magazines on the subject. "He must have seen that there were shortcomings in her education."

By the beginning of 1983, Britain's tabloid press was suggesting that Diana, looking increasingly pale and underweight, was on the verge of a nervous breakdown, symptomatic of an unsteady marriage and overly demanding work schedule. There again, the fact that her husband appeared to be largely unsympathetic to her plight may have been caused by each of them dealing with a different set of anxieties relating to their respective roles.

Dr. Dorothy Rowe, a specialist in stress and depression, and the author of several books on the subjects, observed that the obvious pressures of a job only become stressful if an individual feels that he or she cannot cope with them. "Princess Diana could have suffered anxiety since she assumed her royal duties because she may have felt that she didn't have the background to do them well," she explained.

Camilla Parker-Bowles has often been romantically linked to Prince Charles.

"Prince Charles, on the other hand, [may have been] concerned about his ability to be as good a royal as his mother.

"If you feel good about yourself, then when you encounter a situation that you are either not practiced in or demands a good performance, you will regard this as a challenge which you can and will master. However, if you don't have much self-esteem, then the same situation will become frightening, and this is what causes stress."

Buckingham Palace, meanwhile, together with the usual "close friends" so favored by Fleet Street journalists, responded to media speculation by putting out signals that both Princess and marriage were doing fine. On one matter, however, it appeared that there was agreement in all quarters: There were explosive arguments between the royal couple, with the battle lines being drawn between the Prince's volatile temper and his wife's iron will.

A typical example of this occurred in November 1982, when both Charles and Diana were expected to attend the Annual Festival of Remembrance in honor of Britain's war dead at the Royal Albert Hall in London. On this particular evening, Diana announced that the sleepless nights she had been spending personally attending to baby William had left her completely exhausted, and she would therefore be staying at home. Charles insisted that she change her mind in light of the importance of their engagement. She refused, allegedly explaining that "My duty lies above my loyalty to you."[1] The irate Prince stormed off alone and announced to other members of the royal party that his wife was not well, and her seat was removed from the royal box at the Royal Albert Hall. Yet it appeared that Diana had a sudden change of heart. Taking into consideration the people whom she would be letting down, she arrived at the venue 15 minutes late.

Another, somewhat quieter spat took place in the back of the same royal box. Charles was not only furious at the way in which his wife had made him look, but she had also broken with the established protocol of the monarch arriving after, and leaving before, anyone else. It was not long, of course, before episodes such as this inevitably filtered through to the offices of news editors who, needless to say, immediately made them into headline news. Rumors of a marital rift spread like wildfire, and stories that the Price of Wales had more than met his match in the form of his sweet-faced yet fiery Princess abounded.

At Christmastime in 1983, the BBC ran a 50-minute documentary entitled *The Princess and the People,* covering a year in the royal life and showing Diana's first overseas tour, visiting Australia and New Zealand. What it failed to include, however, were the backstage arguments that preceded the Prince and Princess of Wales' departure for this trip to the South Pacific. Princess Diana insisted that nine-month-old William accompany his parents on the six-week trip.

The Princess did not believe that the task of bringing up her child should be entirely delegated to a nanny and so, in the name of good relations, the Queen consented to this. She also agreed to the unconventional request that her grandson fly on the same plane as her son and daughter-in-law, risking the loss of two future monarchs should a tragic accident take place. As things turned out, the tour went very well, and although Diana was exhausted from the action-packed schedule during which she was able to spend very little time with her baby, she returned home pleased with the enthusiastic reception that she and Charles had received.

On Valentine's Day, 1984, came the official announcement that the Princess was pregnant again. "I haven't felt well since day one," she confided shortly afterward. "I don't think I'm made for this production line."[2] This was an expression she would utilize again, for, in spite of having originally declared that she wanted to have five children, it soon became clear that, for the time being at least, Diana was making do with two. "I'm not a production line, you know,"[3] she reiterated in 1985.

Prince Henry Charles Albert David— otherwise known as Harry—was born on the

Charles and Diana had very different ideas on how they
wanted to raise their children.

afternoon of Saturday, September 15, 1984,
precipitating even wider cracks in the royal
marriage. While Charles reduced his number of
public engagements in order to devote more
time to his family, the matter of the children's
upbringing became yet another subject of
conflict between the parents. Prince William
had proven to be an extremely active,
demanding child, and his father believed that
mother Diana should be stricter in curtailing his
wild ways.

Right from the start, the young Charles had
been raised and trained as a future king, a sense
of duty instilled in him along with the rules of
proper etiquette. This was the way in which he
felt his own successor to the throne should be

handled. In contrast, Diana had been used to an altogether less restrictive atmosphere that gave freer reign to her youthful energies and instincts. Her ideas on parenthood contrasted considerably with those of her husband. He was looking at a future monarch, while all she chose to see was a young child, and so once again the old conflict between traditional and modern values came to the fore.

As things turned out, Prince Harry was an altogether gentler, more withdrawn child than his outgoing older brother, and therefore less inclined to try his father's patience. Nevertheless, the parents squabbled over the education of the boys and their own respective degrees of influence and control. The result was that Charles would eventually win out on the former subject, while Diana would manage to hold sway on the latter when her husband was away on his royal duties.

Charles had initially wanted the young Princes to be raised by his childhood nanny, Mabel Anderson, and a governess employed to look after their education for the first few years within the confines of Kensington Palace. Diana saw to it that they associated with other children first at Mrs. Mynor's nursery school close to central London and then at the nearby Wetherby School in Notting Hill. The main bone of contention, however, was Di's reluctance to pack her children off to boarding school at the age of eight as had been the case with both herself and Charles. She wanted to preside over them as long as possible, at least until the age of 12, but her husband was having none of it. In spite of the fact that he had hated his school-boy days away from home, he was determined to see his sons receive proper training without the undermining influence of their mother's pampering. He used his position as heir to the throne to pull rank in this matter, turning the futures of the two Princes into an affair of the state. Both Princes were to be sent off to the Ludgrove School in Berkshire when they reached the age of eight.

In retrospect, such power struggles only served to widen the rift in the royal marriage and make their life together more unbearable. Lady Colin Campbell, in her book, *Diana in Private: The Princess Nobody Knows,* quoted a relative of Charles as saying, "At times, the tensions between the Prince and Princess have been so great that he has had to get away from her. If he didn't, he'd do something he'd regret, or make himself ill. That's why he's sometimes away from the boys for long stretches ... It's the only way he can cope and still remain married to her."

From all this, it would appear that Diana had been unwilling to abide by all the rules of her royal obligations right from the start. She was just not interested in the monarchy's longstanding role within society, its dependence on public support for its future survival, and the importance of sticking to a tightly regimented way of life in order to attain this. What could the well-bred Lady Spencer have been thinking when she entered into marriage with the future king of England? Did she expect a man so steeped in the traditions of his role to neglect some of his duties and come around to her way of thinking? If so, she really was far more naive than even the press had perceived.

With an institution as well established as the British monarchy, no newcomer can come in and swiftly set about changing the rules of the game, as Sarah Ferguson also discovered. Times may have changed and the hemlines of the Queen's dresses may have been altered accordingly, but the royal call of duty and code of conduct remained fairly constant during her reign. And the Queen will see to it that they will continue as they are for as long as she is around.

This, however, points to another factor that strained the marriage of Charles and Diana. He had long been frustrated about waiting in the wings to assume the royal crown and fulfill his royal destiny. For decades, his mother continually refuted any notion of stepping down to make way for a younger figurehead. The Prince was therefore denied the chance of pursuing the job for which he spent his entire life rehearsing and being trained. Yet, his predecessors, such as Edward VII and the uncrowned Edward VIII, made the most of such periods of waiting by living the high life. Charles, on the other hand, always felt more obliged to honor his public duties. He spent a great deal of time and energy in his work for the underprivileged and stirring up debates on such topical subjects as modern architecture and the environment.

It became the view of many royal observers that after turning 40, the Prince of Wales no longer desired actively adapting his lifestyle toward becoming king. Indeed, after the mid-eighties and especially in light of his then-deteriorating marriage, Charles seemed to be following his own course, including a life very separate from the Princess.

In 1985, in order to preserve some semblance of a proper public image (and silence the ever-increasing tide of rumors and speculation about their relationship), the couple agreed to give a 45-minute television interview. It was broadcast in Britain by ITN on October 20, under the title *In Person, The Prince and Princess of Wales* and edited down to 25 minutes for its airing on ABC's *20/20* on November 7. Sitting together in the drawing room of Kensington Palace, they good-humoredly talked about their work and their happy life together. Diana, coached in advance in the art of clear

Diana was very popular with these Honda employees during her 1990 trip to Japan.

elocution and a relaxed appearance by film producer, director, and actor, Sir Richard Attenborough, talked confidently about her roles as wife, mother, and working Princess. The thoughtful-looking Charles tried to dispel rumors about his eccentricities, such as attempting to contact the spirit of his late uncle, Lord Mountbatten, with a Ouija board.

Overall, the couple appeared to be relaxed and charming. They hoped that his personable appearance would put a stop to all the tabloid gossip about the Prince's strange ideas and his

Fergie provided Diana with younger friends and a more carefree view of life.

wife's temper tantrums, overly demanding nature, and high-spending habits. Unfortunately, however, the problems behind the scenes were beginning to manifest themselves in public.

During their 1986 tours of Austria, Canada, and Japan, Diana appeared openly bored with her husband's philosophical speeches and frequently angry, most notably during the three-day trip to Vienna when the wife of the city's mayor, actress Dagmar Koller, flirted outrageously with Charles at a gala dinner. In Vancouver, where the royal couple opened Expo '86, Diana fainted and slumped into her husband's arms. This episode prompted further speculation as to the state of her health and a denial that she was pregnant. According to a report by *Daily Mirror* correspondent James Whitaker, her exhaustion led her to be bad-tempered with photographers following her every step on the subsequent tour of Japan. Charles tried his best to support her. "No woman could have a more caring and understanding husband," Whitaker wrote, "but even the Prince cannot paper over all the cracks that have begun to appear in his wife's persona."

Yet in the book, *Diana in Private*, Lady Colin Campbell claimed that at around the same time these words were appearing in print, Charles resurrected his relationship with old flame and constant friend, Camilla Parker-Bowles. On discovering this, Diana justifiably threw a fit, but her reaction only had the effect of driving Charles even further away. It was during these troubled times that the Princess sought some fun and lighthearted relief by becoming friends with Sarah Ferguson, the vivacious daughter of Charles's polo manager, Major Ronald Ferguson.

"Fergie" possessed a devil-may-care attitude that provided a welcome change from all the stuffy formality of the old-style courtiers to the royal circle, and she encouraged Diana to be more relaxed and to not always be concerned whether she was doing "the right thing." Diana invited her to join the royal party at Ascot in June 1985, where Fergie met Prince Andrew, leading to their romance and eventual marriage in July 1986. Once she was installed as the Duchess of York, her liberating effect on the Princess of Wales became quite apparent.

Fergie introduced Diana to her own set of younger, more socially uninhibited friends, who were all viewed by the Palace with some degree of apprehension. Lulu Blacker, former girlfriend of the notorious high-flyer, Jamie, Marquis of Blandford, for example, was happy to tell the newspapers about her loves and her dabbling with drugs. Charles and his courtiers were quick to try to put some distance between these people and his family. They did not always succeed. At Ascot in June 1987, Lulu's behind was jovially poked with umbrellas by the Duchess and the Princess—all of which the cameras captured. Diana was then heard to say, "Let's get drunk," as they headed for the restaurant. The end result of that insignificant episode, which in other circles would have been harmless, was a fair bit of damage to the royal image.

Put into context, the episode occurred after several months of hardened press reporting about other less-than-majestic frivolities. On Prince Andrew's stag night, for example, Diana, Fergie, and comedienne, Pamela Stephenson, attempted to crash his party disguised as policewomen. Unsuccessful, they instead spent the night at a nightclub called Annabel's, drinking champagne and orange juice until the early hours of the morning when they returned to Buckingham Palace and stopped Andrew's car as he drove through the entrance.

At a Christmas party held in the Waterloo Room at Windsor Castle, Fergie and Diana danced the can-can together. The two "Throne Rangers," as they were then being described, further upset the royal applecart during a photo session on the first day of a group ski trip at the Swiss resort of Klosters. While other members of their party did their duty and posed patiently for the horde of literally scrambling photographers, the two giggling girls threw snowballs, stepped on each other's skis, and tripped each other up. Charles was clearly embarrassed by the incident, which he instinctively knew would rebound in their faces, and he brusquely advised them to, "Come on, come on!"

The women saw nothing wrong in socializing with and behaving like "normal people"—people outside of the royal circle with whom they could be seen having a good time, laughing, and joking. After all, they were young and had access to friendships with the rich and famous, so why not make the most of this privilege? Consequently, Diana began making new friends of her own, playing tennis with them at the Vanderbilt Racquet Club in London's Shepherd's Bush, and going out more often to various clubs and restaurants.

Charles, on the other hand, found that he had little in common with his wife's upbeat friends, while she had a similar lack of regard for his friends, whom she considered to be bookish types like him. Apparently, however, not all of the Prince's friendships were based on solely intellectual grounds. As mentioned before, of course, there was his chief confidante, Camilla Parker-Bowles, as well as socialites such as the Marchesa di Frescobaldi, Patti Palmer-Tompkinson, Candida Lycett-Green, Lady Sarah Keswick, and Eva O'Neill.[4]

Meanwhile, according to various sources, Diana's circle of confidants and companions grew larger, taking in, among others, King Juan Carlos of Spain, Sergeant Barry Mannakee, and Princess Alexandra's godson, Philip Dunne. The long-distance friendship with King Juan Carlos remained, while Mannakee was, for a short time, Diana's bodyguard and her closest friend in times of despair. He was not, however, of noble stock, and when eyebrows started being raised, the Palace saw to it that he was transferred away from the Royal Protection Department. That was in July 1986. In July 1987, an accident tragically claimed his life.

The same year, the Princess encountered the handsome, well-to-do merchant-banker Dunne, and he began joining her and Charles on the

This Majorcan vacation with King Juan Carlos of Spain and his family was fun for everyone. Rumor had it that the King and Diana were close friends.

ski slopes at Klosters and inviting her to stay at his family home, Gatley Park in Herefordshire, while his parents were away. She accepted, and the gossip columnists had a field day when Dunne turned up as a member of the royal party at Ascot, and was then seen to be enjoying himself at a wedding party for the Marquis of Worcester. At this affair, Diana was seen running her fingers through his hair and kissing him on the cheek while the two danced the night away together. This was in full view of the assembled guests. Charles, however, did not take any notice as he spent the evening engrossed in conversation with Camilla Parker-Bowles, before leaving alone late at night.

Needless to say, the national press went wild. Stories abounded with reports on how the royal couple spent their sixth wedding anniversary apart. In October, the Prince flew down from Balmoral to Scotland to join Diana in Wales to visit victims of a flood in Carmarthen. The two had not seen each other for the past 30 days, yet the atmosphere while they were together was fairly icy. As soon as the visit was over, Charles went back to Balmoral, where his houseguests secretly included Mrs. Parker-Bowles.[5] Now the tongues really began to wag and with good reason. It was as if the heir to the throne was making it plain for the world to see that he could not bear to spend longer than was absolutely necessary with his wife. There were now only token gestures to maintain the pretense that they were not leading separate lives.

Amid the intrusion into their private lives by the media (with which Diana often felt she could not cope), the Princess sought out her own brand of publicity. During the first five years of her marriage, she had been the undisputed center of attention on the world celebrity stage. After the arrival of the Duchess of York on the scene, she had been somewhat upstaged. Having formerly taken the ever-present photographers for granted and often pressured into resenting them, she now did an about-face and defensively—if mistakenly—asserted "You won't need me any more, now you've got Fergie."[6]

It seemed that as soon as she was faced with the threat of being edged out of the limelight, Diana's ego took a severe bruising, and she needed to reassure herself that she retained people's love and attention. Quite simply, she wanted to remain number one. To meet her goal, she contrived ways in which to be the center of attention in front of the cameras and to be front-page material for the newspapers and magazines.

In August 1986, while vacationing with King Juan Carlos and Queen Sofia in Majorca, Charles was annoyed that the paparazzi had managed to take photos of his wife in a bikini. Later that year back at Balmoral she apparently made concerted efforts to appear with her sons in front of the ever-prying lenses. As reported in Sally Moore's book, *The Definitive Diana*, after visiting the Arab Gulf States that November, she modestly told journalists, "Oh, you should have seen some of those Arabs going ga-ga when they saw me on the Gulf tour. I gave them the full treatment and they were just falling over themselves. I just turned it on and mopped them up."

In February of the following year, the Prince and Princess took a trip to Portugal, where, as the tabloids noted, they slept in separate four-poster beds in adjoining rooms at the Queluz

Palace. According to *The Definitive Diana,* while attending a banquet at Lisbon's Ajuda Palace, she flirted with the country's 62-year old president, Dr. Mario Soares. "If I get cold, will you warm me up?" She inquired, before responding to the offer of his dinner jacket by pulling on his suspenders (called "braces" in Britain) and teasing, "You're a socialist, aren't you? You should be wearing red braces!" Evidently, this kind of behavior did nothing to help her cause.

Again, it is difficult to ascertain precisely what motivated Diana to behave in this way. She surely knew that she was overstepping the mark that had been clearly defined for her. Were her actions simply intended to make the Prince jealous and to revive his attentions? Or did she want to humiliate him in public for his coldness to her in private? Was the Princess so insecure that, in spite of all the attention that was lavished on her by people wherever she went, she needed to witness it demonstrably on a one-to-one basis? Or was all this just her way of displaying her independence, of not bowing to royal convention, and of doing things her own way?

Whatever the reason, she soon learned that such behavior was in no one's best interests. She was the real loser, since each incident was graphically reported and the public reaction was one of irritation more than admiration. The

Duchess of York, having been placed on the obligatory pedestal by the media during the early days of her royal liaison, was now being criticized by the same media hounds for her pompous attitude. Diana realized that her own flighty remarks and gestures had to stop if she was going to hold on to her own position as the "Top of the Royal Pops." Even her astrologer, Penny Thornton, whom she had been consulting closely during 1986, advised her to toe the royal line and not get herself into any trouble.

With Charles hardly acting as a paragon of virtue himself, the Queen was quickly getting tired of the bad publicity the younger generation of royals was producing. In her usual fashion, she took care of the problem quickly and efficiently. The Queen made it clear to all those concerned that she was not amused and that all those concerned had better shape up fast.

Her immediate concern was gossip that cast her oldest son's marriage in a bad light. There were strong rumors that both he and the daughter-in-law were summoned and told that even if they could not be hospitable toward one another in private, they should at least get their public act together. They were instructed to put on a happy face and try to be seen together, instead of openly pursuing separate lives with other companions.

Whether this meeting actually took place or not is difficult to confirm, but what is certain is

The travels of Charles and Diana took them
to many exotic places.

that Philip Dunne was contacted by the Palace
and instructed to stop seeing the Princess of
Wales. The clear message was that in the future
there would have to be more discretion shown
all around.

Yet judging from their behavior, it appears
that Charles and Diana did not take the
Queen's alleged edict too seriously. There were a
few sporadic attempts to present a united front,
but these often appeared halfhearted and failed
to really convince much of anyone.

At the end of a polo match during a tour of
India, the Prince tried to plant a kiss on his
wife's cheek and ended up looking at the back

of her neck. Did she turn away on purpose? Or was he just careless? This could well have been just an innocuous incident that the photographers capitalized on, but there were times when it appeared that while the royal couple felt duty-bound to make an effort, their frustration with the situation in which they had become trapped became the stage on which they acted out their dislike for one another.

With Philip Dunne pushed into the background, Diana's next confidante came in the form of Captain James Hewitt. A member of the Life Guards, he met the Princess when she started giving her, William, and Harry horseback-riding lessons after being posted to Combermere Barracks near Windsor. While Diana found his straightforward, dignified manner and keen sense of fun a big help in her battle against loneliness and depression, the boys also liked the attention he gave them at a time when they were not seeing much of their father. The four of them spent several happy weekends together with James Hewitt's parents at their home in Devon. Of course, the royal family was not too happy about the children getting attention from a fill-in father. When newspapers and society magazines began to pick up on this, the Queen once again took action to limit the damage to the royal armor. The result: The relationship with young Hewitt was cooled.

In March 1988, Diana became involved in the work of RELATE, a relationship guidance organization of which she eventually became patron. With her experiences as the product of a broken home and the victim of a disintegrating marriage, she probably felt a particular alignment to this group. She set out to learn from the difficulties of others, as well as to offer her own assistance and advice to those in need.

"When Diana first became involved in 1988 we were celebrating our Golden Jubilee, and we asked Diana to become involved as our patron," recalled RELATE'S Chairwoman, Zelda Westmeads. "At that point, she was heavily committed, and she never takes on commitments unless she can give full support. Then, a year later, we were very honored when she accepted."

"Diana's work with RELATE . . . led her to think about her own situation, and talk it over with other people and start to change," said Dr. Dorothy Rowe, who was a regular worker in this organization. "She is not just [about] royal hand-shaking, but . . . sitting in on counseling sessions and case studies, and you can't listen to that kind of discussion without relating it to yourself."

The same month that she began working with RELATE, Diana needed all her powers of caring, understanding, and communication to deal with the tragic death of Prince Charles's

The death of Major Hugh Lindsay was a blow to both
Charles and Diana.

close friend, Major Hugh Lindsay. Di was with
the Duchess of York in the royal party's rented
chalet in Klosters when they learned that
Lindsay had been killed in an avalanche, which
had narrowly spared the life of several others,
including the heir to the throne. Distraught and
upset, Diana drew upon her inner resources to
hold herself together and insisted that they
must return home immediately. Charles had
wanted to continue the vacation. The fact that
she had managed to keep a cool head in a crisis

when others had momentarily lost theirs instilled in her a new sense of purpose and confidence. At a time of tragedy, Diana rediscovered her inner strength, which helped her to start looking ahead—a skill that she would soon put to use.

On the day of the Princess's 30th birthday, July 1, 1991, the media picked up on the fact that no official celebration had been arranged to mark the occasion. Fingers were immediately pointed at her uncaring husband, who evidently was not interested in the celebration. His loyal friends, in an attempt to protect the Prince, jumped to his defense and informed Nigel Dempster, a gossip expert for *The Daily Mail,* that Charles had offered to throw his wife a party, but that she had turned him down.

Once again, two clearly defined camps with differing ideas came to the fore, leading to even more speculation about the state of the Wales' marriage. Subsequent joint appearances quelled some rumors during the next few weeks. Even more fires were doused when Charles and Diana, on a Mediterranean cruise aboard a yacht owned by shipping billionaire John Latsis, appeared to be both friendly and affectionate to each other. The relationship of the royal couple seemed less strained for a while, as they appeared to settle into an acceptable form of public lifestyle. Then, on March 29, 1992, while they and the children were on a skiing holiday in the Austrian resort of Lech, the Princess learned that her father, the 8th Earl Spencer, had died. She wanted to return home alone, but Charles insisted that, if for no other reason than public relations, he should fly back with her.[7] This was the last thing that Diana wanted to deal with in her hour of grief, leading to yet another battle of wills. Once again, the Queen's word ruled. She insisted that the Princess travel with her husband.

A united front was presented to the waiting reporters and photographers at the airport. After arriving back at Kensington Palace, Charles moved on immediately to Highgrove, from where he flew two days later to join his wife at the funeral. By May, they were vacationing separately again—she on an official visit to Egypt, and the Prince on a "sketching trip" to Turkey. And in June, all pretenses of a working marriage were blown to bits when Andrew Morton's book, *Diana: Her True Story,* hit the stands.

Among Morton's revelations were allegations that Diana had been close to calling everything off two days before the wedding. At this time, she discovered a gold-chain bracelet that her fiancé insisted on giving to Camilla Parker-Bowles. The bracelet allegedly bore a blue enamel disc with the entwined letters "F" and "G"—Fred and Gladys being the Prince's and Camilla's pet names for each other. Also, on their honeymoon Charles supposedly wore a pair of cuff links in the shape of two intertwining "Cs" given to him by Camilla.

Another shocking revelation was the reason for Diana's sudden weight loss after their marriage. Morton maintains that this was a symptom of the early stages of her ten-year struggle with *bulimia nervosa,* a disorder in which massive eating binges are interspersed with periods of fasting or induced vomiting. But the biggest shock of all was the contention that a result of the mood swings that follow the binges and the state of her marriage had led Diana to such depression that she attempted suicide five times. The princess apparently cut her wrists with a razor blade, threw herself against a glass cabinet at Kensington Palace, cut herself with the serrated edge of a lemon slicer, stabbed herself in the chest and thighs with a penknife, and threw herself down a full flight of stairs at Sandringham House when she was three months pregnant with Prince William. Examinations by doctors confirmed that the baby had been unharmed.

Episodes such as these were apparently cries for help rather than serious attempts to take her life, but at the very least they certainly appeared to have been expressions of frustration. "When a lot of women purposely cut themselves, it is often because they feel powerless to change things or influence situations," explained Dr. Dorothy Rowe. Nevertheless, the Prince of Wales apparently showed little concern or inclination to help in this matter.

Andrew Morton, a 38-year-old former tabloid reporter who had written several books on the royal family, stated that Diana's inner circle of friends, family, and counselors had cooperated with him in providing both source and photographic material for her biography. They "believed that for once the truth should be told about the difficult life Diana has led," he wrote. Suspicions immediately arose as to the cooperation of Diana herself in the project. Morton said that in return for slanting the book in her favor, he found himself being granted interviews by friends who always check with the Princess of Wales before talking, which is not very often.

"I very quickly came to realize that you choose which side you are on—his or hers," Morton told Newsweek. "If I had tried to straddle the divide between them, word would have gotten back to the Palace and doors would be closed." To prove that Morton's facts were correct, Diana's friends who had spoken to the author announced after the book's publication that he had correctly conveyed what they had told him. Furthermore, while the Palace issued a statement asserting that the Princess had not personally granted Morton any interviews, there

Diana was told of her father's death while on a skiing holiday in Lech, Austria.

was no official denial of the stories contained in the book.

On June 7, the day that excerpts from the book debuted in the London *Sunday Times*, Camilla Parker-Bowles—referred to by Diana as "the rottweiler" according to Morton's book—and Camilla's husband, Andrew, sat in the royal enclosure at Windsor Great Park to watch a game of polo. In an apparent show of solidarity, she was invited to tea by the Queen. "I'm certainly not going to bury myself away because of what the papers say," Camilla told the assembled reporters afterward. "Absolutely not. Why should I?"

In the meantime (interestingly), senior executives of Harrods, London's "top people's store" described the Morton book as a "scurrilous publication" and banned copies of it from their shelves. The Archbishop of Canterbury, Dr. George Carey, urged the rampant British press to exercise some restraint, expressing concern for Princes William and Harry who were caught in the middle. He also added that the royal family was in his prayers. However, it was Diana who at that time appeared to require his prayers the most. While visiting a cancer hospice on June 11, she openly broke down and wept when she saw supporters carrying signs that said "We Love You."

At the same time, the world's press was doing its very best to stir up the debate. In

Australia, public interest was at such fever pitch that thousands of people called in to a hotline number in order to hear royal marriage updates. Back at Sandringham, officials had to put up velvet ropes to keep onlookers away from the staircase from which Di purportedly flung herself when she was pregnant.

Meanwhile, the Prince and Princess made their first public appearances together since the scandal broke, standing side by side on the balcony of Buckingham Palace for the annual Trooping the Colour festivities on June 13. They did the same at Windsor Castle for the traditional Order of the Garter ceremony two days later and at the racecourse during Royal Ascot week. During this time, another crisis conference was reportedly convened between the Queen, Charles, and Diana at Windsor Castle. Once again, it was agreed that not only would the couple put on a show of unity in public, they would also try to do so in private whenever their sons were around, in order to minimize the effect that the marital troubles were having on the children.

Subsequently, on June 17, it was announced that Diana's schedule of forthcoming public engagements, which had been blank in precisely the same manner as Fergie's prior to her separation from Prince Andrew earlier in the year, was filled up. A couple of joint appearances for her and Charles and a trip with

Diana, seen here with Charles and her sister Sarah, took her
father's death very hard.

him to Korea in November were scheduled.
Then, on June 21, the two of them dressed up in
cowboy costumes and joined in the fun and

games at a party thrown by Greece's ex-King Constantine, at his home in the north London neighborhood of Hampstead Garden Suburb. The party was thrown to celebrate the tenth birthday of Prince William and the ninth of Constantine's daughter, Theodora. In marked contrast to previous joint appearances, the royal couple looked relaxed and happy.

So it seemed that officially, at least, nothing had changed, and the two sets of opposing supporters slugged it out in public. "We are in danger of losing the Princess of Wales," had been Andrew Morton's dramatic warning on the front page of the *U.K. Today* on June 15. "The Prince of Wales, the Royal Family and the establishment are doing nothing to help her in this moment of crisis," he stated, before appealing to the public to apply pressure on the royals so that Diana would get the help she so desperately needed.

This view was backed up by Stephen Twigg, who was reportedly visiting the Princess at least once a week for "psychological counseling and massage." He indicated that without a specific resolution to the ongoing melodrama, Diana would experience a rapid and serious decline in health. "The situation has to end or there will be a tragedy," he exclaimed.

Yet in the same newspaper four days later, Maya Parker, a leading Harley Street (London) therapist who had "counseled countless famous clients with similar problems to Diana's," contended that the only person who could resolve the problem was the Princess herself. Mrs. Parker informed readers that Diana's disrupted childhood had prevented her from growing up. She was "a naughty teenager, and whatever her sweet public image, she can be a very nasty one, too."

In her "detailed assessment of the case," Parker also cited Di's sanctioning of friends to reveal her secrets through the Morton book as "a sixth suicide attempt, designed to tell Charles and the royal family, 'Now the whole country will listen to me.'" This kind of behavior, however, would have no lasting benefit, asserted Mrs. Parker. "Instead of throwing herself downstairs or seeing astrologers, she must seek the right kind of help," she astutely observed.

These views aside, it should also be noted that if the Princess had used Andrew Morton's book as a means of airing her grievances, her conduct could also be perceived as not so much a sign of weakness or juvenile behavior as one of strength and increased maturity enabling her to take a new approach in dealing with her problems. "As people mature, they often learn that you can still get your own way, but you can be a lot more clever about it," said Dr. Dorothy Rowe. "It's about being pro-active rather than reactive."

Whatever the truth, the Di, so to speak, had been cast.

CHAPTER 3

CHARLES: THE BACHELOR HUSBAND

I n order to even begin to understand the motivations and actions of Prince Charles, it is necessary to gain some insight into his boyhood years. He is, after all, a human being who was conceived and born in the same manner as anyone else, yet his existence once he had left the mother's womb was beyond comparison. It was his unique life, primarily during the formative years, which sets him apart; it was in isolation that the roots of his personality were formed and his character was shaped.

Privilege may be enviable to the masses who have never known it, yet to someone who is accustomed to no other way of life it is the norm, an isolated existence where advantages are taken for granted, and obligations and

Prince Charles takes his status as future King of Britain very seriously.

expectations, which accompany all of the benefits, are often a real burden.

This is not the story of a Hollywood upstart, an offspring with access to great material wealth and social opportunities, who can live in the shadows of the parents' fame, seek to emulate it, or develop as a celebrity in his/her own right. Instead, it is the tale of a child who is bred as a pedigree, cultivated and trained to assume a role of great social importance but little political significance. It is the life of a boy raised in a sheltered environment full of tradition, pomp, and circumstance, but with little relevance to the outside world. It is the epitome of an outmoded existence in a modern world.

Right from the start, the future monarch was marked as different from the rest. This little boy saw his face reproduced on postage stamps and was accustomed to the public being interested in his every move. While such matters were accepted as routine, and the duties and responsibilities of the royal family were instilled in his young mind, Charles felt increasingly alone as the years progressed. Many of the reasons for his feelings of seclusion lay with his own parents.

When at around 9:15 P.M. on November 14, 1948, the future Prince of Wales became the first royal to be born at Buckingham Palace in 62 years, 21-gun salutes were fired. The British

As a child Charles spent very little time with his mother, since she was often away on royal duties.

people, living fairly hard lives in a country still attempting to pick itself up from the effects of World War II, celebrated by dancing in the streets and lighting bonfires. This baby, after all, was the first direct male successor to the throne since the uncrowned Edward VIII.

Crowds stood outside the Palace all through that rainy Sunday, excitedly waiting for news as a string of well-known doctors passed through the royal gates. Inside, while the first-time mother was enduring the tribulations of childbirth, her husband was displaying no qualities of patience. By early evening the whole air of expectancy had made Prince Philip so edgy that he went away to swim and play squash in another part of the Palace with his good friend, Lieutenant Commander Michael Parker. It was on the squash court that Sir Alan Lascelles, private secretary to King George VI, told him of the good news.

The fact that Philip was absent at the moment when the future King entered the world would prove to be a taste of things to come. The child—soon to be named Charles Philip Arthur George—would see very little of either his father or his mother during his formative years.

The first 12 months were not so bad, with Philip based at the Admiralty in London and Princess Elizabeth close at hand. As time went on, however, Philip was involved in active naval duty, while Elizabeth was allotted more royal assignments as her father's health deteriorated.

On August 15, 1950, Princess Elizabeth gave birth to her second child, Anne. It was now in his younger sister's company that Charles spent

Charles, seen here with his sister Anne, was apparently a shy a serious child.

most of his days under the tutelage of nannies, Mabel Anderson and Helen Lightbody. Their mother's daily schedule would include half an hour with them each morning and then, whenever possible, another couple of hours toward the end of the afternoon. It certainly did not amount to much time together!

Even within the closest family circle there was a distinct air of formality. The young boy was taught to bow before receiving a kiss from his great-grandmother, Queen Mary, and to stand, unless permitted otherwise, when in the presence of his grandfather, the King. These were the relatives Charles saw most, since his parents—especially his father—were spending more and more time away from home. George VI, suffering from cancer, was embarking on his final, fairly rapid decline. While he was confined to staying at home and subjected to a series of operations, he had to delegate more and more of his royal duties to his oldest daughter and son-in-law.

By July 1951, Prince Philip had to give up his naval command in order to commit himself full-time to working with the Princess. On February 6, 1952, while staying at a hunting lodge called Treetops next to Kenya's Sagana River, an aide fell to one knee and addressed Elizabeth as "Your Majesty." The 25-year-old knew that she had become Queen Elizabeth during the night. Her father had succumbed to the effects of his heavy smoking at the premature age of 56. She now had to totally devote her life to her royal duties.

At Easter of the same year, the monarch and her family moved into Buckingham Palace from Clarence House, where the King's wife and their younger daughter, Margaret, were now to live. Life initially proceeded along similar lines for the small Charles, but as time wore on, he began to notice some not-so-subtle differences. After all, he now had his own car with his own private chauffeur, his own footman, and the first in a long line of ever-present private detectives who would accompany and watch over him for the rest of his life. He also assumed the formal title of the Duke of Cornwall.

While experiences like those on the day of the Queen's June 1953 coronation—when he and his family stood on the Palace balcony and waved at the massed crowds—made him more accustomed to public attention and adulation, the heir to the throne was, unlike his gregarious younger sister, a shy, sensitive child. During his earliest years he may have tried to act like his father, but it soon became clear that he did not share his character.

Sometimes away from her children for up to six months at a time while she was away on tour, the Queen had noticed that the combined effects of her lifestyle and his upbringing were producing a growing sense of nervousness and confusion in Charles. Therefore, instead of thrusting him from his sheltered environment straight into the outside world, she chose to have his first formal education administered by a governess, Catherine Peebles, in the privacy of an allotted room at Buckingham Palace.

The Queen also tried to keep him away from the prying eyes of the media. Her press secretary issued statements appealing to the news hounds for restraint and decorum whenever the Duke of Cornwall and his governess visited public places, such as museums, in the course of his education.

In Britain, an heir to the throne had never attended a normal school, but by the fall of 1956 Queen Elizabeth felt that the time was right to break with the centuries-old tradition. She wanted her son to start mixing with other children of his own age in a nondomestic environment. This began gradually, with Charles still being taught at home by Miss Peebles in the mornings, before joining his class at Hill House private school in London's Knightsbridge each afternoon. The following year, he went there on a full-time basis. The teachers addressed him as "Prince Charles," while the pupils were allowed to dispense with the title.

In the meantime, the boy's relationship with his father added to his feelings of confusion. The Duke of Edinburgh was a forceful, opinionated man who believed in strict training for his son. He punished him whenever he stepped out of line and attempted to raise him as a true man of the world in the best male chauvinist tradition. While Philip tried unsuccessfully to coach him in the art of boxing and hoped to see him excel at team sports such as cricket and soccer, Charles was clearly far more adept at the gentler, solitary pursuits of fly-fishing, soccer, swimming, reading, painting, and watching television.

Philip's influence may have been omnipresent, but the man himself was often away on official duties. This switch in atmosphere was very difficult for young Charles to adjust to. The situation became even worse when his parents decided to send him to a private boarding school in 1957. They felt this experience would give him the best education, in an environment suitably protected from the intrusions of the media.

Like most children his age, Charles was reluctant to leave home. But he, of course, had no say in the matter and in September of that year he and his parents arrived at Cheam, the old-fashioned institution that Philip himself had once attended. On the train journey from Balmoral down to London the night before, the young Prince was literally trembling with nerves before being driven to the village of Headley where the school was located.

Newsreels of the time show a solemn little boy walking straight as a rod with hands behind his back, raising a cap to his teachers, and generally behaving in a manner associated with an army general. Charles's private detective would remain with him at the school, but as soon as his parents had departed, a heavy depression set in. He would look back on his first days at Cheam as the most miserable of his early life.

Gradually, however, he began to mingle with the other boys. In spite of the Queen's expressed wish that her son be treated just like

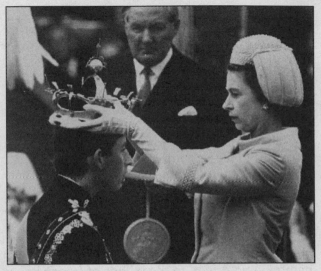

Charles was crowned Prince of Wales on July 1, 1969, the day Diana turned eight years old.

anyone else, given his fame and social position it was almost impossible for him not to be the center of attention. Added to this was the problem of press photographers making a nuisance of themselves. Journalists actually offered pupils bribes in order to gather any little piece of information that could be turned into a sensationalist story.

Once again, the Queen's press secretary had to intervene. At the end of the first semester, newspaper editors were warned that they either stop this nonsense or the Prince would have to be withdrawn from the school and educated within the confines of Buckingham Palace. They agreed, but the pressure was beginning to show on Charles, who felt that with all eyes focused on him he had to always appear "interesting." He withdrew even further into himself.

There was also the matter of following in his father's footsteps. Philip had not exactly proved himself to be the brain of Britain during his stay at Cheam—nor at any other time, for that matter—and Charles performed likewise. Of course, complimentary reports would find their way into the newspapers about him being "bright" and "above average." The truth is that while history and geography were his favorite subjects, he just plodded along in others, and was poor in math and foreign languages.

Whereas Philip had been good in cricket, rugby, and soccer, Charles was bored by the first activity, poor at the second one, and, although he eventually managed to become captain of the school's soccer team, his side lost every single game. The team scored a grand total of four goals all season. This boy was not his father's son!

Prince Philip, however, was still inclined to impose both his opinion and his authority wherever and whenever he deemed necessary. Charles had just about started to come to terms with Cheam when it was time for him to move on. Conscious of the fact that he was still homesick, the Queen had assumed that his next port of call would be Eton, the traditional bastion of the upper class conveniently situated very close to Windsor Castle.

The Duke of Edinburgh, on the other hand, had an entirely different plan in mind. Staying near the family's weekend residence would, the Duke insisted, only make his son an easy target for the press. Philip believed that it would therefore be much wiser for Charles to study just about as far away from home as was possible while still remaining in the British Isles. The perfect place for this would be Gordonstoun, Scotland, where Philip himself had once been a pupil! Charles was eager to please his father and therefore went along with the idea, but this was a decision he would sorely regret.

If sports had been a boring nuisance at Cheam, at Gordonstoun they were a constant hardship. Physical fitness was the priority here, with mountain-climbing, firefighting, life-saving, challenging assault courses, long runs, and cold showers all part of the accepted regimen. If a boy did not go along with this, then he would be admonished by his superiors and shunned by his peers.

Worse still, trying to blend in with an entirely new bunch of teenagers with his reputation (and a private detective to boot) was a harrowing experience. Compared to the reaction of the little children when he had joined his previous school, the "young men" of Gordonstoun were not about to try to befriend Charles. Many of them, in fact, kept their distance, compelling the student Prince to while away his leisure hours wandering on his own along the blustery North Sea coastline.

At an age when most young people are forming new friendships and exercising an increasing amount of freedom, the future King was feeling increasingly more trapped and isolated. Even the press seemed to be against him. An innocent incident of the 14-year-old Charles trying to order a cherry brandy at a local bar was made into a major event. This experience left deep emotional scars and a lasting mistrust of the press. All in all, by the end of 1963 Charles hated his school.

Vacation times spent at home were not necessarily joyous, either. The Prince of Wales regularly clashed with his father, often ending up crying in response to one of Philip's overbearing lectures or criticisms. There were rumors that on one such occasion Charles steeled himself and plucked up the courage to remind the Duke of Edinburgh that he was talking to the future King of England. Philip reportedly walked out of the room.

The next year was not much better, with magazines publishing extracts from his stolen English essay book and then unjustifiably claiming that the Prince himself had sold this to a classmate when he needed spending money. Academically, however, things were looking up, and by 1965 he had passed "O" levels—the regulation "ordinary level" exams, usually taken at the age of 16. He had passed the required tests and could move on to higher education in English language, English literature, Latin, French, history, and math. He had also, by virtue of his acclaimed performances in school music and drama productions, received greater acceptance from the other students.

Hereafter, life improved dramatically. Charles's parents allowed him to take an extended hiatus from Gordonstoun in order to study at Timbertop, in the Australian outback. Located in the remote foothills of the Victorian Alps, 200 miles to the north of Melbourne, the students learned to fend for themselves, hunting, cooking, woodcutting, organizing their own schedules, and looking after the younger boys. Charles flew out in January 1966, and immediately felt at ease with the way of life there.

Living in a hut compound, he did his fair share of the household chores and joined in activities ranging from long-distance runs and cross-country hikes to felling trees, shearing sheep, and panning for gold. He also had to put time aside to study for the "A" level exams

As a student at Trinity College in Cambridge, Charles studied anthroplogy, archaeology, and history.

(higher education "advanced level"
qualifications required to enter college), which
he would be taking on his return to England.
On his Australian adventure, however, Charles
endeared himself even more to his Australian
hosts by placing less emphasis on his academic
work than on his outdoor activities.

For the first time in his life, Prince Charles
felt as if he had been accepted not for what he
was but for who he was. Away from the
claustrophobic atmosphere contrived by the
British press, he was only too happy to stay on
for a second semester. On the other hand, when
he did have to face a big crowd gathered to
catch sight of him, he now found that he had
the confidence to talk and mingle with people.
He would never forget his time in Australia.

Back within the comparatively boring
confines of Gordonstoun, the "born-again"
Prince developed his tastes for opera, classical
music, and archaeology. He also passed "A"
levels in French and history, making him the
first-ever British heir to the throne to have
qualified for university studies by conventional
means. Also, having reached the age of 18, he
could now, if necessary, ascend to the role of
King of Britain without the need for a stop-gap
regent.

His newly acquired skills of self-sufficiency
came in handy when Charles arrived at Trinity
College, Cambridge, in October 1967, to begin

his three-year degree course in archaeology and anthropology. At a time when the youth movement of the western world was taking a trip through "flower power" and drug-induced psychedelia, here was a youth who was more interested in the ancient than the modern, Bach than the Beatles, and Shakespeare than Sartre. This was also the era when student revolts against the establishment were at their peak, and if anyone was symbolic of the old order, it was the Queen's son.

Consequently, Charles surrounded himself with polo-playing, landed gentry types. He immersed himself in intellectual, economic, and political discussions with both them and the college master (and former Conservative government minister) R. A. Butler. After his first year, he studied history, before royal duty called and the future King had to obey, studying Welsh for a month at the University College of Wales prior to his investiture as Prince of Wales on July 1, 1969 (coincidentally, the day of Lady Di's 8th birthday).

In 1970, having celebrated his own 22nd birthday, Charles completed his history course at Cambridge and emerged as the first-ever heir to the throne to have gained an honors degree. With his newfound confidence, he would spend the next few years immersing himself in the role of a "man of action"—flying jet fighters and bombers to earn his RAF wings, and serving

Skiing is one of Prince Charles's favorite sports. Here he is
seen at Klosters, Switzerland.

diligently in the Royal Navy aboard nuclear
submarines and vessels such as the HMS
Norfolk, HMS *Minerva,* and HMS *Jupiter.* During
this exciting period, he would learn firsthand
about the qualities of comradeship and bravery,
and experience the rewards of carrying out
hard, yet rewarding tasks.

This, then, was the man whom Lady Diana
Spencer would one day agree to marry, "for

better or for worse." This was a man of varied experiences who had managed to struggle through the oppressive obstacles of his early life, and in the process developed a strength of character and clarity of vision. He now acknowledged that the right kind of formal discipline can help properly shape a person's character during the formative years, laying solid foundations for the long road ahead.

Also, as time passed, he would come to firmly believe, as did his father before him, in the traditional aristocratic ways of raising children, instilling in them a strong sense of social responsibility, and delegating their upbringing to others when duty—or preferred pastime—called. "Charles's rather difficult relationship with Philip during his early years may have distorted what could have been a better understanding of his own sons' needs," said leading royal observer Margaret Holder. "He has some strange notions about how much time he should spend with them, and he has totally failed to grasp that a month away from them is a long time." This was a man of independent will, strong belief in himself, and fair intellect, who now embraced tradition, believed passionately in the role that birthright had allotted him, and placed his duty to his country above all else.

His background and outlook were in marked contrast to that of the future Princess of Wales.

CHAPTER 4

YOUNG DIANA: GROWING PAINS AND ADOLESCENT ANGST

The Honorable Diana Frances Spencer literally had problems from the moment she was born—early in the evening on Saturday, July 1, 1961. The little 7 lb. 12 oz. bundle of joy was, at that moment, a profound disappointment to her parents, the Viscount and Viscountess Althorp, otherwise known as Johnnie and Frances.

Not that there was anything wrong with her physically—far from it. The simple matter was that after seven years of marriage the Sandringham-based aristocrats were still hoping for the obligatory son and heir to the title. Without one, the Spencer earldom—and all of

As a teenager Diana was a very friendly, outgoing girl who was always around to help anyone in need.

the associated riches—would be lost to other, more distant relatives. Nine months after their marriage, their first attempt at having a son had resulted in the March 1955 birth of Sarah. Then in 1957, there was Jane. When in January 1960, a boy finally did arrive, the family was struck by tragedy. Baby John died a mere ten hours after his delivery, an incredible blow both psychologically as well as emotionally. As a result, the parents' powerful mixed feelings of anguish, hope, and profound desperation were so intense by the time their next child came into the world that they were convinced it was going to be a boy.

They had not even bothered preparing themselves for the alternative. When the baby was born in an upstairs bedroom at Park House, they suddenly found themselves in the position of having to come up with yet another girl's name. This lack of preparation, as well as their barely disguised disappointment, was also evident when the child was christened at St. Mary's, Sandringham, on August 30, 1961. Whereas the oldest sister Sarah's godmother was Queen Elizabeth, The Queen Mother, and Jane's godfather was the Duke of Kent, young Diana was accorded no such distinction. She had to do with a collection of the family's high-society friends, relatives, and neighbors. Little did they realize that one day this same little girl would become the first Englishwoman in 300 years to marry an heir to the throne.

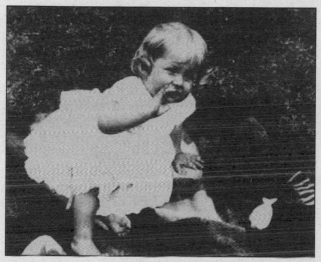

On her first birthday Lady Diana did not appear to be the least bit shy.

While Charles and Diana were already cousins several times over and had a common royal ancestor in King Charles I, she was the one who had far more British blood running through her veins. She was descended from King Charles II through different lines, all of them illegitimate, courtesy of the kings' mistresses: Frances, Countess of Jersey, with George IV; Barbara Villiers the Duchess of Cleveland, Louise de Keroualle the Duchess of Portsmouth, and Lucy Walter with the obviously overworked Charles II; and Arabelle Churchill with the

Duke of York (later James II). Di was, in fact, also related on her father's side to legendary wartime prime minister, Sir Winston Churchill, but the famous connections hardly stop there.

Her close and distant cousins also include another former prime minister, Sir Alec Douglas-Home (Baron Home of the Hirsel), as well as Oliver Cromwell, Bismarck, Lawrence of Arabia, King Juan Carlos of Spain, and the Aga Khan. Writers Jane Austen, George Orwell, Samuel Pepys, George Sand, Graham Greene, Erle Stanley Gardner, Louisa May Alcott, Ralph Waldo Emerson, Virginia Woolf, and Barbara Cartland; philosopher Bertrand Russell; painter John Singer Sargent; and missing noble Lord "Lucky" Lucan are all relatives.

Then there are the likes of U.S. presidents George Washington, Calvin Coolidge, and Franklin D. Roosevelt; celebrities such as Rudolph Valentino, Lillian Gish, Humphrey Bogart, Orson Welles, Olivia de Havilland, and Lee Remick; tycoon Nelson Bunker Hunt; heiress-cum-jeans designer Gloria Vanderbilt; and former *Washington Post* editor-in-chief Ben Bradlee.

For all her steeping in the British aristocracy, Diana's ancestry has strong roots in the United States of America. It may also be this side of the former family that endowed her with her well-known stubborn streak and hot temper. Her great-great-grandfather, Frank Work, started out as a clerk in Ohio during the 19th century and went on to make millions as a Manhattan stockbroker. All of the wealth, however, brought with it the power to impose his will on those around him. In line with his hatred of foreigners, he threatened to cut his children out of his will should any of them marry someone who was not American.

At the top of his most-hated list were aristocratic Europeans. So when his daughter Frances—known as Fanny—decided to cross the Atlantic to marry James Roche, the future 3rd Baron Fermoy, a family rift ensued. The marriage broke up ten years later, and when Fanny returned to the States with her twins Frank and Maurice and daughter Cynthia, Frank, Sr., forgave her on the condition that she would not do the same thing again. He even extracted an agreement that her children would remain in America and become U.S. citizens within 12 months of his own death.

In 1905 the cycle repeated itself when Fanny ran off with and married Aurel Batonyi, a Hungarian racehorse trainer in her father's employ. After divorcing him four years later she once again returned and her father once again forgave her. (They were nothing if not consistent!) Frank, Sr. died in 1911, yet as soon as he did, his Harvard-educated grandchildren contested his will on the grounds that grandpa had been "unduly prejudiced against

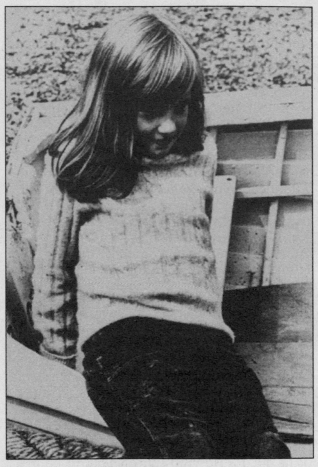

Diana, here on vacation at Itchenor, Sussex, was a sweet
child who loved the outdoors.

foreigners," and the family inherited his $25 million fortune.

When Fanny's first husband died in 1920, their son Maurice Roche ascended to the title of the 4th Baron Fermoy and settled permanently in Britain, where he became a Tory member of Parliament and mayor of King's Lynn. In 1931, at the age of 46, he married the 20-year-old Ruth Gill, the daughter of a Scottish army colonel, who had been studying at the Paris Conservatory of Music when they first met. Her family was of decent if not grand stock, even though great-grandmother Katherine was the product of an unwed liaison between a worker for the East India Company and a girl from Bombay. In those days, this was the stuff of family secrets.

In any case, when Baron and Lady Fermoy married, King George V offered them a home at Park House on the Royal Sandringham estate in Norfolk. It was here that Diana's mother Frances, was born on January 19, 1936.

Di's father, Johnnie, on the other hand, was some 12 years older. A godson of Queen Mary, his family comprised a line of earls, dukes, and duchesses stretching back to the 15th century. The title of Earl Spencer was bestowed on one of Johnnie's ancestors by King George III. It was thereafter passed down through successive generations until it reached Jack Spencer, who married the beautiful and sweet-natured Lady

Cynthia Hamilton, daughter of the Duke of Abercorn and the grandmother from whom Diana is thought to have inherited her looks.

Their son Johnnie, was educated at Eton and Sandhurst, which proved to be a welcome break from his father's cruel, sadistic nature and violent temper. After fighting for the Royal Scots Greys in World War II, he spent three years in South Australia as Aide-De-Camp to the Governor. A good looking, amiable man, who on occasion acted as escort to Princess Margaret when making up a foursome with Princess Elizabeth and her husband, Prince Philip, Johnnie became equerry to King George VI in 1950. Through his position, he was the natural choice for the role of Master of the Queen's House when the King died a few years later.

While he was unofficially engaged to Lady Anne Coke of Holkham Hall, Viscount Althorp met and fell in love with the 18-year-old Frances Roche. When they married on June 1, 1954, Frances became the youngest bride to walk down the aisle in Westminster Abbey in this century. This was the biggest society wedding of 1954, attended by 1,500 guests including the Queen, Prince Philip, the Queen Mother, and Princess Margaret. When Baron Fermoy died the following year, Lady Ruth Fermoy handed over Park House to her daughter and son-in-law.

During the next ten years and despite all the misery and heartache of waiting for the successful arrival of a son and heir, Frances and Johnnie retained a very strong physical attraction for one another. Intellectually, however, they were learning that they were not nearly as compatible.

Frances was a sophisticate—a bright, elegant, fun-loving woman with a sharp sense of humor and an appreciation of the arts. Johnnie, on the other hand, was becoming increasingly dull and boring in her eyes. He was an uncomplicated man of little ambition, who preferred hunting on his Norfolk estate to socializing in London with his wife. Worse still, while he was kind and affectionate toward his children, he could also be opinionated and argumentative with his wife. Frances often felt that he was taking her for granted.

The incessant pressure that they both felt to sire a male heir hardly helped matters. Even though this was alleviated when their son, Charles—godson to the Queen—was born on May 20, 1964, Johnnie was by then managing to unwittingly irritate Frances in almost every way, and she was beginning to look for a way out of the unpleasant relationship.

Even though the marriage was falling apart, their children were nevertheless enjoying a happy, balanced childhood. There was a nanny to look after them and six servants to take care of the ten-bedroom house with its outdoor swimming pool, tennis court, cricket pitch, and

Taking care of children was always one of Diana's favorite
activities. Here she is seen with two of her young charges
from the Young England kindergarten.

staff cottages. The home atmosphere was warm,
and informal. Diana loved it here, and her
earliest memories are of roaming the grounds,
surrounded by a veritable menagerie of
animals.

Her education began at the age of four. A
governess, Gertrude Allen (known as Ally), took
charge of a group of a dozen or so local children
who would gather each day in a room at Park
House. This was next to what was fondly

referred to as "The Beatle Room," where every available inch of wall and floor space was adorned with posters and other Fab Four-related items. Other than that upper-class concession to the four superstars, the children's whole lifestyle was reminiscent of a bygone age. During these years, they never realized that theirs was a privileged, unusual existence, even if they were sometimes visited by the likes of Princes Andrew and Edward.

When the arguments between Frances and Johnnie began to increase both in volume and frequency, the atmosphere went into sharp decline. At times like these Diana would try to keep out of their way, afraid that she might be a nuisance and, perhaps, the cause of their fights. In reality, nothing she could either do or say was about to save the Althorps' doomed marriage.

The turning point came at a friend's dinner party in 1966, when the couple encountered Peter and Janet Shand Kydd. Peter, a handsome entrepreneur and former naval officer, was the virtual opposite to the Viscount Althorp. He was bright, witty, ambitious, and generally exciting to be around. He and Frances were immediately drawn toward one another. A friendship was struck between all four and soon they went on a skiing vacation together.

It was here, while spending the nighttime hours chatting away with Johnnie Althorp, that

Janet Shand Kydd realized her husband's interest in Frances had extended beyond drinks and laughter. The Viscount, however, was blissfully unaware of what was going on and would remain so until it had become common knowledge to just about everyone around him.

When they returned from vacation, Frances and Peter began meeting in secret at Queen's Gate in the fashionable London neighborhood of South Kensington. By the following summer, it became obvious to everyone including Viscount Althorp that both marriages were over. Peter decided to leave his wife and three children. Shortly after Diana's two older sisters, Sarah and Jane, had departed for West Heath boarding school that September, Frances packed her bags and left Park House to move into a rented apartment in London's exclusive Cadogan Place, Belgravia.

In spite of the stories that were later circulated, stating that the Viscountess had deserted her husband and children without prior notice, this was not true. In fact, Diana and Charles joined her at the Belgravia apartment the very next day. Diana was soon enrolled in a day school, while Charles went to kindergarten. The Althorps had agreed to a trial separation. In the meantime, the children still visited Park House on weekends and the whole family got together there during half-term and at Christmas in 1967.

By this time, however, Frances knew that there was no chance of resurrecting the marriage. When Johnnie realized this, he decided to play the part of Scrooge rather than Santa. He insisted that the children remain permanently at Park House with him and continue their education at Sillfield School in King's Lynn. Frances pleaded and objected, but her husband would hear none of it. He was determined that his children would not live under the same roof as their mother and her lover.

Left with no alternative, the Viscountess started legal proceedings to gain custody of the children and dissolve her marriage, citing "cruelty" by her husband. On April 10, 1968, Janet Shand Kydd sued Peter for divorce on the grounds of his adultery with Frances in April 1967. In June, the Althorps' custody hearing took place in the Family Division of the High Court prior to the divorce itself.

In Britain, children are invariably placed in the woman's care unless she either does not want them or is judged by the court to be an unfit mother. Adultery does not come into this decision. Since Frances had neither neglected nor battered her children, she justifiably expected to gain custody of them. But there were two factors that she did not bargain for: First, her husband's title cast him in a favorable light with the court and second, there was the unbelievable intervention of her mother, Lady Ruth Fermoy, who actually gave evidence against her own daughter in the proceedings. The nobility had closed ranks.

Needless to say, with this kind of support from her nearest but not dearest, Frances lost the case, the children, and any respect that she had for her mother. She never forgave her for this betrayal.

In April 1969, Johnnie was granted a divorce on the grounds of his wife's adultery, and the following month Frances and Peter got married in a registry office. While the dust began to settle around the adults, the children started reaping the adverse effects of all the bitter recriminations. Diana became uncharacteristically rebellious and hyperactive, while she tended to the maternal needs of her little brother, Charles, who missed his mother terribly. At the same time, Jane withdrew more into herself, and Sarah routinely scorned any kind of discipline, on one occasion bringing her horse into the drawing room.

Regular weekend visits to see their mother only caused more upset. Frances would frequently break down and cry at the thought of them leaving the next day, and this in turn incited them to be even more difficult to handle when they returned home. Their father and grandmother, who had been so determined to oust the children's mother from the scene, now found themselves barely able to cope with the responsibility that they had taken on. They just could not bring back the happy, upbeat atmosphere that had permeated Park House when Frances was there.

Adding to these problems was the sudden high turnover of nannies. Some of them had been fired for mishandling the children; others had quite simply had their patience tried to the limit and could hardly be blamed for wanting to leave. From the children's point of view, they regarded any new female face who walked in the door as being a potential replacement for their mother. Determined to prevent this from becoming a reality, Diana, Jane, Sarah, and Charles would act up and misbehave as much as possible.

All in all, life was not exactly a bowl of cherries for anyone concerned. Many of the children's personal problems as adults would be diagnosed as symptomatic of the trauma that they experienced during this crucial period. Certainly it could account for Diana's feelings of loneliness and insecurity, her need for attention, and her eating disorder. If so, this is just the typically ironic result of actions taken by parents "in the interests of the children."

Eighteen months after her parents' divorce, Diana was, like her sisters before her, sent to boarding school. Riddlesworth Hall in Norfolk resembled a large, aristocratic country house. It

Even as a teenager Diana was known for her style in dress and her outgoing character.

trained upper-class girls to become well-bred young ladies, briefed in the routines of etiquette and proper behavior. The educational program was made up of traditional subjects such as English language, French, Latin, classic English literature, history, math, geography, and science. There was also the opportunity to pursue hockey, volleyball, tennis, swimming, and ballet.

After initially resenting being sent away and viewing it as a sign of rejection, Diana took to Riddlesworth as home away from home or even as a welcome reprieve from home. She was a popular, helpful, outgoing student who made a number of friends among the 120 girls. But at the same time, she always felt slightly separate from the rest. Nevertheless, at the end of her first year at Riddlesworth, her headmistress, Elizabeth "Riddy" Ridsdale, awarded her the Legatt Cup for her helpfulness.

Di excelled at physical-education activities—winning cups and captaining teams. The academic classes were another matter. She longed to be as bright in the classroom as her sisters Sarah—whom she idolized—and Jane; even her little brother, Charles, would one day study at Oxford University. While she wrote imaginative essays in English and enjoyed studying history, it soon became clear, especially to Diana herself, that she was just not good at schoolwork.

Diana's grandmother, Countess Spencer, died of a brain tumor in 1972. Despite her loss, the following year 12-year-old Diana did pass her Common Entrance exam and was admitted to the £3,000 ($5,700) per semester West Heath boarding school, where both Sarah and Jane had already studied. A large Georgian mansion, set in 32 acres of rolling Kent countryside, West Heath would provide Diana with some of her closest and most enduring friendships, though it did take her a while to adjust. After only six weeks there she was so miserable that she arrived back home in tears and was only persuaded to stay on at the school when her Australian headmistress, Ruth Rudge, encouraged her to "develop her own mind and taste."[1]

At least she was asked to return, which was more than could be said for her sister, Sarah, who was suspended from school when her rebellious, often outrageous behavior—which included a penchant for drinks of the stiff variety—could no longer be tolerated. Sarah did, however, manage to pass six "O" levels (the regulation "ordinary level" exams, usually taken at the age of 16, as the required qualifications for moving on to higher education in selected subjects). Jane, whose reserved, dependable character was in marked contrast, passed 11 "O" levels.

When Diana tried to pass five "O" level exams (in English language and literature, history, geography, and art), she failed all of them. A second attempt to do better only resulted in a single, second-grade pass in art. Her other qualities of friendliness and caring, on the other hand, were noted and regarded. By the time she left West Heath in 1977, Di had been promoted to school prefect and awarded the Miss Clark Lawrence Award for service to the school.

Back home, all was not well in the Spencer household. In June 1975, their grandfather had died, precipitating their father's elevation to the title of the 8th Earl Spencer. Charles adopted the viscount Althorp mantle, the three girls became ladies, and a move from the beloved family home at Park House to the Spencer residence at Althorp soon took place.

Originally established in 1508 by Sir John Spencer, a sheep farmer who became one of the wealthiest men in England, it was later altered by architect Henry Holland in the late 18th century. Althorp was a large, magnificent house surrounded by a 600-acre park on a 13,000-acre estate just over an hour's drive north of London. Inside, the many huge rooms were populated with some of the finest antique furniture and paintings in the country. Incredible crystal chandeliers reflected off the marble floors, and stunning tapestries lined up along with works of Gainsborough, Reynolds, Van Dyck, and Rubens.

Diana could not help but be charmed and fascinated by all that she saw, while in her spacious second-floor bedroom she happily whiled away the hours delving through her large collection of Barbara Cartland books. Little did she or the other children realize that in a short time they would, in fact, be related to the romantic novelist, and that the cause of this would lead to some very unpleasant repercussions.

Cartland's oldest child and only daughter, Raine, Countess of Dartmouth, began having an affair with the new Earl Spencer soon after he and his family had moved to Althorp. The following year, 1976, her husband, Lord Dartmouth, sued for divorce citing the Earl for adultery. Shortly after, on July 14, the love match was sealed at Caxton Hall registry office in London. None of the Spencer children were in attendance at the wedding. They quite simply had not been told about it—and with good reason. More than likely, they would not have wanted to go.

A tall, imposing woman, with the gaudy, overstated dress style of her famous mother and a bouffant hairstyle to match, Raine came to Althorp with a solid reputation for being as extroverted and overbearing as she was sharp.

As a Tory adviser and then as a member of the British Tourist Authority, she gained a lot of tabloid exposure by complaining about the dirty teacups of Heathrow Airport. After her marriage to Johnnie, she quickly set out to "update" the Spencer home with funds accrued from the sale of some of the paintings and other treasures—an act viewed by some as a disgrace. It was opened up as a tourist attraction to ensure that it could remain a self-sufficient enterprise. Also, outspoken, often hurtful remarks, meant that she successfully alienated most of the Althorp inhabitants.

It is never easy for a stepparent to fit in with a existent family unit, since the children often resent the intrusion of a "replacement." In this case, however, Sarah, Jane, Diana, and Charles had made it clear from the start that they would have rather seen their father marry anyone but her. Needless to say, it did not take long before a deep-rooted mutual animosity set in.

"Raine stopped play," was a popular saying around the Althorp grounds, as was "Raine, Raine go away." Meanwhile, the servants were not exactly having an easy time of it. After a couple of kitchen hands were tactlessly described by Countess Spencer as "a pair of sluts," they were heard to remark, "It never Raines, but it pours."

While Jane acted as if her stepmother didn't even exist and quite literally ignored her for

This young-looking Diana certainly had no idea how
complicated her life would become one day.

about two years, Sarah was openly rude and
hostile toward her. Even the usually compliant
Diana and Charles took it upon themselves to
repeatedly defy and annoy her. Raine's
subsequent retaliation was to publicly describe
Jane as "Only good for producing children,"
Sarah as "Okay while she sticks to hunting and

shooting which is all she cares about," and, regarding Diana, "How can you have a conversation with someone who doesn't have a single "O" level? It's a crashing bore."

Relations would remain strained throughout the years. While the Spencer children all adored their father—whom they were annoyed to hear being addressed as "Johnnikins" by their stepmother—the girls began to spend less and less of their time at Althorp. While still at West Heath, Diana started to stay in London with her sisters on weekends. She left England in January 1978 to enroll in domestic science, dressmaking, and cooking classes at the Institute Alpin Videmanette, an exclusive Swiss finishing school in Rougemont near Gstaad, which Sarah had previously attended.

Di was meant to learn to speak French during her stay there, but she and her friend, Sophie Kimball, spent most of their time speaking English and having fun racing down the ski slopes. After six weeks, Diana grew bored with the lack of social life in Rougemont and yearned to return home. After going back for a vacation she decided to stay in England at the London home of her mother Frances, rather than at the Raine-swept abode of her father.

At the ripe old age of 16, Diana Spencer was defining a new lifestyle for herself and searching for a means to support it.

CHAPTER 5

A FINE ROMANCE: THE COURTSHIP AND ENGAGEMENT

When Diana first met her husband-to-be, she was still a shy and innocent 16-year-old student at West Heath, whereas he was just about the world's most famous—or famously—eligible bachelor. In November 1977, they were introduced to one another in the middle of a plowed field near Nobottle Wood on the Althorp estate during a weekend pheasant shoot.

The person responsible for engineering this encounter was none other than Di's volatile oldest sister, Sarah, who at this time was in the middle of a nine-month romance with the Prince of Wales. Sarah had started seeing Charles socially a few months earlier, and in February of 1978, she joined him on a skiing

The engaged couple looked quite happy in 1981 when they attended a performance at Goldsmith's Hall.

vacation in Klosters, Switzerland, prompting brief press speculation that the two would soon be walking down the aisle together.

Yet on that fateful November weekend, it was not only Sarah who was attracting the good-time Prince's attention. For while Diana may have thought that her sloppy clothes and slightly overweight figure would hold little appeal for him, it was her unusually outgoing behavior at a dance that her parents had thrown in Charles's honor that ignited his interest.

"I remember thinking what fun she was," Charles would recall in an interview at the time of their engagement. "What a very jolly, amusing, and attractive girl, great fun, bouncy, and full of life."

The two, however, did not meet again for a full year. At this point, we'll have to improvise the next part to their story, Diana, we know, was immediately taken with the Prince, but never gave her chances a second thought. As for Charles, on the other hand, we can opt for the romantic scenario in which our hero is unable to get the young girl out of his mind, but has to wait for the right opportunity to see her again. We should, however, opt for the most likely but less interesting version in which he continues to pursue his happy-go-lucky lifestyle without giving her another thought. Either way, Charles remembered her sufficiently to invite both Di and Sarah to his 30th birthday bash at Buckingham Palace in November, 1978.

By this time, the relationship between the Prince and the older Lady Spencer was over, and his belle for the ball was the attractive blonde actress, Susan George. Once again, Diana enjoyed herself in the royal company without ever considering the possibility that she may be in line for some princely attention. She continued on the course that she had been carving out for herself since quitting Swiss finishing school at the beginning of the year and moving to London.

Her first job of any kind was away from the bright lights and big city, however. For three months she stayed at the Hampshire home of family friends, Major Jeremy and Philippa Whitaker, cooking, cleaning, and caring for their six-year-old daughter, Alexandra. Then she returned to her mother's Belgravia apartment and, while the Shand Kydds were residing in Scotland, shared the place with friends, Laura Greig and Sophie Kimball.

Diana also started undertaking a number of odd jobs offered to her by both family and acquaintances. People she knew found her work as a cocktail waitress at private parties, a baby-sitter, a cook, and a £1($1.90)-per-hour cleaning lady. She earned her keep, even though apart from the occasional restaurant meal, she hardly ever spent her money on discos or other teenage haunts. A quiet evening in the company of friends or sitting at home reading and watching television were the regular leisure activities during this period. She became more mobile after passing her driving test the second time she took it.

In September of 1978, Diana decided that she needed to acquire some marketable skills with which to pursue a full-time career. She attended Elizabeth Russell's ten-week cooking course in Wimbledon (southwest London).

That same month, trouble hit the Spencer family. Her father suffered a near-fatal stroke. The Earl was still having difficulty hanging on to life at the Brompton Hospital in South Kensington when his daughters, Di and Sarah, attended Prince Charles's 30th birthday party in November.

Raine maintained a bedside vigil and, despite her almost-daily clashes with Sarah, she gradually helped nurse him back to health. He eventually left the hospital in January of 1979 and led a full and happy life, although he never recovered from a slowness of movement and a slight slur in his speech.

In the meantime, Di had completed her cooking course, gained a diploma, and been assigned jobs preparing and serving food at parties given by an agency called Lumley's. She was just drifting and did not work too hard. Next came a brief stint as a £100 ($190)-per-year student ballet teacher at the Vacani Dance School in South Kensington. Here she enjoyed honing her own skills as well as helping in classes for children aged two to nine. This so-called career was short-lived. After falling and injuring her left ankle during a French skiing vacation in March 1979, Diana never returned to the studios of Miss Betty Vacani.

Diana returned to a string of cooking and cleaning jobs while still sharing her mother's home with her roommates. Then, on her 18th birthday on July 1, 1979, the youngest daughter of the 8th Earl Spencer inherited the handy sum of about £60,000 ($114,000) from her American great-grandmother, Fanny Work, whose will had already provided for Sarah and Jane. Di's mother wisely suggested that, like her sisters, she should invest her inheritance in property. Within a week she had found a place that she liked, a spacious £50,000 ($95,000) three-bedroom apartment on a 1920s red-brick mansion block situated in a fashionable area between South Kensington and Fulham.

Coleherne Court would soon become the base and focus of intense media attention when the royal spotlight would be turned on its new young inhabitant. Before she could ever imagine what was about to happen, Di set about spending some of the remaining money from her inheritance on totally modernizing and refurbishing her new home.

Diana and Charles posed for this happy photo after the
official announcement of their engagement.

After the remodeling was completed, she was joined in her luxury apartment by friends Carolyn Bartholomew, Sophie Kimball, and Philippa Coaker. The latter two were eventually replaced by Anne Bolton and Virginia Pitman. The three tenants each paid their teenage landlady £18 ($34) per week. Diana supplemented this income with a job helping to supervise small children at the Young England kindergarten in St. Saviour's Church Hall, Pimlico (southwest London).

Diana worked at the kindergarten three afternoons a week. Deciding that her income was insufficient, she signed up with such aptly named employment agencies as Universal Aunts, Solve Your Problems, Knightsbridge Nannies, and Occasional Nannies. In November 1979, she got an extra £1 ($1.90)-per-hour part-time job at the Battersea (south London) home of a Mr. and Mrs. Jarman. A couple of months later, she was hired to baby-sit an American oil executive's son two days a week.

These odd jobs enabled Diana to have a dress allowance at Harrods, maintain a car—a Honda Civic that would later be replaced by the renowned sky-blue Volkswagen Polo—and socialize around town in the style of a "Sloane Ranger." She fit in perfectly with well-to-do "Hooray Henrys" and "Hooray Henriettas" of the British upper class, so named because of their reputation for hanging around—and throwing lavish parties at—the bars, clubs, and restaurants of exclusive London areas such as Sloane Square. It was in the company of a number of such platonic male friends that Diana would frequent these places.

This was the girl whom the Prince of Wales would soon be seeing an increasing amount of. A lively young aristocrat, still occasionally shy and apt to blush whenever someone attempted to engage her in conversation, Diana was now also beginning to come out of her shell thanks to her new-found independence and expanding social circle.

Charles, on the other hand, was a future King, a man in his early 30s who had enjoyed the benefits of his privileged position and was still enthusiastically playing the field. He was also the oldest-ever bachelor Prince of Wales and, as such, duty-bound to find himself a wife and produce an heir.

Charles was perfectly happy leading the single life. He was an independent-minded man with a lifelong reputation for being something of a loner. He was not in desperate need of the kind of support, sharing, and familiar companionship that a stable relationship brings. Instead, he was content to be footloose and fancy-free, able to indulge himself to his heart's content without having to compromise his pleasures out of consideration for the needs and desires of a permanent partner.

As we have already seen, if Charles did have a strong sense of commitment, it was to his predestined role in life. When the pressure of his parents, palace courtiers, and great-uncle and mentor, Lord Louis Mountbatten, began to be turned up for him to find a future Queen, he felt obliged to comply. The murder of his beloved "Uncle Dickie" (his pet name for Mountbatten) that same year, at the hands of IRA bombers, only increased this feeling.

The search was therefore on, and as the world's press busied themselves speculating about the bridal prospects of the various "Charlie's Angels," the Prince diligently utilized his resources of energy and judgment in order to ensure that he would make absolutely the right choice.

"I think that he was undoubtedly a Casanova," says Margaret Holder, one of Britain's leading royal observers and a regular contributor to magazines and books on the subject. "Much was disguised and withheld from the public at the time, but he had regular meeting places with girls; Lord Mountbatten had allowed him to use his Broadlands residence to court ladies, and he also used various other private homes.

"He's supposed to be an incurable romantic, although a late starter—it wasn't until university

Prince Charles and Lady Diana apparently did not know each other well enough when they got married.

that the interest in women took hold. Much has only come to light in later years, but he had a longer list of girlfriends than Prince Andrew, who was nicknamed 'Randy Andy' by the press."

Over the years, ever since his first proper relationship with Lucia Santa Cruz during his days at Trinity College, Cambridge, the Prince had indeed been "seen in the company of" a steady stream, of eligible and some not so eligible—women. His love interests have run the whole gamut of the class system and ranged from titled ladies to celebrities.

Familiar-faced companions have included the aforementioned Susan George, as well as Sheila Ferguson, lead singer of the all-female group, The Three Degrees, "Prince Charles's favorite pop group," as the tabloids dutifully pointed out (never mind that he had never previously shown any interest in pop music). These women added to the overall air of glamour and excitement, but they were never really serious contenders for marriage. To put it bluntly, they were "unsuitable types" for acceptance into the highest family in the land.

There were also girlfriends dating back to the early seventies. Among them were Dale Tryon and Camilla Parker-Bowles, who, when married, would become confidantes to the Prince. As for all the others—well, the media speculators came up with a host of likely candidates.

In 1972, there was Georgiana Russell, the daughter of a former Miss Greece and a British ambassador to Spain, now Lady Boothby and living in Wales. Then there was Lady Jane Wellesley, daughter of the 8th Duke of Wellington, who remained the Prince's almost-constant companion for around three years before they each decided to part and go their separate ways.

Next, after a brief encounter with Laura Jo Watkins, whom Charles met when his ship, the HMS *Jupiter*, docked in California in 1975, one of the hottest favorites for the title of Princess of Wales came to the forefront. Davina Sheffield appeared to have the approval of not only the Prince but, more importantly, his closest relatives and even the press. The two started dating in 1976, shortly after Davina had returned from refugee work in Vietnam following the brutal murder of her mother by robbers at the family's Oxfordshire home. Charles fell head over heels for her, but when one of Davina's former lovers sold his story to the newspapers, the image of a potential royal had been irreparably—if hypocritically—damaged and the romantic balloon had to be burst.

Thereafter, in addition to Lady Sara Spencer, others who came and went included Jane Ward, whom the Prince met when she was working in an office at the Guards Polo Club; Sabrina

Guinness, a former acquaintance of Mick Jagger and Ryan O'Neal, whose position as heiress to an Irish brewery made marriage to her out of the question; Lady Amanda Knatchbull, granddaughter of the late Lord Mountbatten; and Anna "Whiplash" Wallace, the daughter of a Scottish landowner, whose nickname was earned courtesy of her quick temper and sharp tongue.

Charles and Anna were both avid hunters, and he not only found Anna exciting to be with, but he was also disarmed by the way in which she seemed to be completely undaunted by his social standing as the Prince of Wales. She regarded and respected him like a normal human being, and, as such, she expected him to respond in kind. She took no nonsense from anyone, and so when, in June of 1978, the Prince spent the entire evening ignoring her and dutifully mingled with all the guests at the Queen Mother's 80th birthday party at Windsor Castle, "Whiplash" stormed out, having told him, "Don't ever ignore me like that again. I've never been treated so badly in my life. No one treats me like that. Not even you."

She was wrong. Shortly afterward, Charles did exactly the same thing at a high society ball in Gloucestershire, when he spent most of the evening on the dance floor with Camilla Parker-Bowles. The quick-tempered Anna once again stomped out, and this time she didn't return.

Anna "Whiplash" Wallace was one of the few people who could stand up to the Prince.

"He always had to be the dominant person in any relationship," asserted Margaret Holder. "Some girls didn't like to be treated in this way, and it often led to a break-up which he himself may have regretted."

This brings us to the point at which the royal gates were opened to Lady Diana Spencer. In January of 1979, she had been invited by the Queen to join family and friends at Sandringham for a shooting weekend, courtesy of sister Jane now being married to the monarch's assistant private secretary, Robert Fellowes. A similar invitation had been extended to join them at Balmoral in July, and on both occasions Diana had shown herself to be warm, witty, fun-loving, and easy to get along with. She was becoming increasingly smitten with the Prince of Wales, too.

She would once again be a royal guest at Sandringham during February of 1980, and in July of that year she was in the party that went to see Charles play polo with his team, *Les Diables Bleus* ("Blue Devils") at Cowdray Park in Midhurst, Sussex. At the Duke of Richmond's Goodwood House Ball, thrown to mark the end of the Royal Goodwood horse race week, many of the guests took note of the way in which Charles and Diana danced so close together, and when, soon afterward, the Prince invited Lady Di to a performance of Verdi's *Requiem* at London's Royal Albert Hall—albeit with her grandmother,

Everyone certainly expected the marriage of Charles
and Diana to be a happy one.

Lady Ruth Fermoy, acting as chaperone—it
appeared that romance could be in the air.

In August, Diana joined the royal family
aboard their yacht, *Britannia,* for Cowes Week,
the annual Isle of Wight event where top
yachtsmen from around the world rub shoulders
with the elite. There she made an impression on
the Prince during a wind-surfing expedition on
the Solent by showing off her figure as she
weaved her way along the river. She also took
the opportunity to drench the heir to the throne
by tipping over the mast of his Windsurfer. The
following month she was in his company again
at Balmoral.

By this time it was clear that their meetings were neither just coincidental nor just invitations from the royal household. Slowly but surely, Charles had been won over by the warmth, charm, sensitivity, and looks of this flirtatious 19-year-old. When the press spotted them together as the Prince fished for salmon in the River Dee at Balmoral, the cat was out of the bag and, at least as far as the tabloids were concerned, a new royal romance—or could it be the royal romance—had commenced.

"HE'S IN LOVE, AGAIN" screamed *The Sun* in its usual understated way on September 8; "Lady Di is the new girl for Charles" was the subhead. Now the floodgates had been opened, and as the fairy tale started to look like an increasing possibility, so Diana had to come to terms with the fact that she was saying goodbye forever to the normal life of privacy to which she had been accustomed.

Of particular convenience to the Fleet Street paparazzi was the proximity of her Coleherne Court home to the kindergarten where she worked. An army of camera lenses was stationed outside the apartment morning, noon, and night. What they did not initially clue into, however, was the service door at the rear of the mansion block through which she would enter and depart, while porters at the main entrance would assure the reporters that she was "about to pass this way any minute."

Making getaways in her pale blue Volkswagen or, after she had crashed that, a bright red Mini Metro, Diana would often get lost in traffic in order to shake off reporters.

After weeks of this relentless pressure, however, the strain began to tell. In December 1980, Di's mother, Frances Shand Kydd jumped to her daughter's defense and wrote a letter to *The Times:* "May I ask the editors of Fleet Street, whether, in the execution of their jobs, they consider it necessary or fair to harass my daughter daily, from dawn until well after dusk? Is it fair to ask any human being, regardless of circumstances, to be treated in this way?" She continued to assert that she agreed with the freedom of the press, but questioned how there could be any respect from the public when none was shown toward it.

All the while, the people actually standing in the eye of this hurricane were each trying to settle their own minds about their future. Diana's feet had hardly been allowed to touch the ground since that Balmoral weekend in September, and so strong was the tide of hype and emotion on which she had been swept that she just wanted to step back for a moment and be able to contemplate the biggest decision to this point in her young life.

"It was a rather stilted romance," explained Margaret Holder. "Charles was calling the shots, and there was always the difficulty of having a courtship away from anyone—either the press or his rather middle-aged friends.

"Even though they were divorced, Diana's mother and father should have advised her against the marriage as she was far too young and too untried. She was a very unworldly 20-year-old. She possibly liked the idea of being Princess of Wales, but was perhaps blinded by him. . . . Love is blind, as they say."

Charles, on the other hand, had to feel sure that this was not only the right girl for him in terms of personality and looks. She had to be capable of handling a role that she had never been trained for. He consulted with aides, asked the advice of his confidantes, and spent long hours mulling everything over in his mind.

On Friday, February 6, 1981, shortly after returning from his annual skiing trip to Klosters, Lady Diana Spencer accepted Prince Charles's proposal of marriage in the nursery of Windsor Castle. The Queen was informed in a telephone call by her son to Sandringham, and the following day his fiancee told her own parents and family. Once she had taken a hard-earned break with her family in Australia and the wedding plans were well under way, the world was informed of the happy news.

It was February 24, 1981, and all appeared to be well.

CHAPTER 6

FAIRY TALES CAN COME TRUE: THE WEDDING

A s the news was flashed to all corners of the world that Charles, Prince of Wales, and Lady Diana Spencer, youngest daughter of the 8th Earl Spencer, would marry at St. Paul's Cathedral in London, on Wednesday, July 9, 1981, crowds gathered at the two main focal points—Buckingham Palace and Coleherne Court. For those hoping to catch a glimpse of Diana in the days to come, however, the Palace would be a far better bet than the mansion block located in The Little Boltons in southwest London. The night before, Diana had left her comfortable apartment behind forever.

Diana was allotted a Rolls-Royce from the Royal Mews to replace the red Mini Metro that had helped her escape the media hounds so

The wedding of Charles and Diana took place at St. Paul's Cathedral in London.

many times these past few months. She was then taken to Clarence House, the London residence of the Queen Mother and her lady-in-waiting, Lady Ruth Fermoy, with Scotland Yard detectives as royal protection. Officially, she would live here until the wedding, with her and Charles's grandmothers paving the way for the big day. Unofficially, according to several sources, she only slept there the night before the wedding.

The overall planning of the whole ceremony was the function of the Lord Chamberlain, yet the Prince's input played a large part in deciding the style and appearance of the occasion. It was, after all, he who announced that the venue for the marriage would be St. Paul's Cathedral instead of Westminster Abbey where royal weddings had usually taken place in recent times. His reason for making this choice was that, in addition to the visual splendor of Sir Christopher Wren's celebrated landmark, Charles had always dreamed of having a musical wedding on a grand scale. St. Paul's spectacular acoustics would perfectly cater to this.

In conjunction with Sir David Willcocks, the director of the Royal College of Music, Charles recruited the assembled talents of three orchestras of which he himself was patron. The Bach Choir, of which he was president, and the vocal talents of New Zealand opera star, Kiri Te

Kanawa, who would soon afterward be made a dame by the Queen, were also enlisted.

As for the actual music, the Prince and his bride would each take three and a half minutes walking up the aisle to the strains of Purcell, Handel, and Jeremiah Clarke. On the way back together, they would be accompanied by the compositions of Elgar and Sir William Walton. The couple's respective choice of hymns for the occasion reasserted the ceremony's religious attributes and social significance. Charles decided on "Christ Is Made the Sure Foundation," while Diana appropriately chose "I Vow to Thee My Country."

Diana, meanwhile, was sporting the magnificent £28,500 ($54,150) engagement ring purchased by Charles (or, some reasoned, by the British taxpayers) from the royal jewelers, Garrard's. It featured a large oval sapphire as its centerpiece and was surrounded by fourteen diamonds set in white gold. This was supplemented by the Queen Mother's gift of the late Queen Mary's diamond and emerald pendant, designed to resemble the feathered emblem of the Prince of Wales.

During the wedding, Charles was to wear his royal navy commander's uniform. The royal fiancée selected David and Elizabeth Emanuel to design her dress, on the strength of a chiffon blouse of theirs that she had worn for a photo session with Lord Snowdon. They in turn came up with a creation in ivory-colored English silk, which was embroidered with pearls and mother-of-pearl sequins, together with massively ruffled sleeves, a V-shaped neckline, and a bodice extensively frilled with lace. The longest-ever royal bridal train measured 25 feet in length. Ivory was selected instead of the traditional white in order to cut down on reflection from camera lights on TV. The fine silk veil with mother-of-pearl sequins was to be complemented by a diamond tiara belonging to the Spencer family.

The matching slippers, meanwhile, were made by Clive Shilton, while the "something old" was the lace that had belonged to Queen Mary. The "something borrowed" were the earrings belonging to Diana's mother, Frances Shand Kydd, and the "something blue" was the small bow sown to her waist along with a tiny gold horseshoe.

The five bridesmaids wore matching ivory-colored dresses, while the two pageboys donned royal navy cadets' uniforms dating back to 1863, the year of the last state wedding of a Prince of Wales, when the future King Edward VII married Alexandra of Denmark. Cut out and sewn single-handedly by Greek seamstress Nina Missetzis, the bridal gown was altered and re-altered in a state of high secrecy during the months, weeks, and days leading up to the wedding. This was largely due to the bride's

Diana's dress had a 25-foot long train, making it extremely difficult to walk or get into the wedding coach.

incessant weight loss. When Diana was booked for fittings by the Emanuels, she adopted the very ordinary pseudonym of Miss Deborah Smythson Wells!

Before her dress had been completed, however, she had to practice her "wedding walk," which Diana reportedly did by pacing up and down the length of the huge St. James's Palace ballroom. She did so dragging yards and yards of paper tissue attached to her head. Because of the large crinoline skirt, Di had to rehearse getting into and out of the glass coach that would take her and Earl Spencer from Clarence House to St. Paul's Cathedral. Her hair would be styled—without hair spray—by Kevin Shanley, while her makeup would he applied by the world-renowned Barbara Daly.

Two thousand six hundred and fifty wedding invitations were mailed out by the Lord Chamberlain and, during the weeks before the wedding, gifts, letters, and postcards arrived from all over the world. President and Nancy Reagan gave a $75,000 cut glass vase, Arab sheiks sent gold ornaments and jewelry, and children in schools all over the United Kingdom sent their paintings and good-luck messages. In fact, in between the announcement of their engagement and the day of the wedding, the royal couple received a staggering 100,000 letters together with more than 10,000 presents.

Meanwhile, the world's press and media people were quite literally falling over themselves and each other trying to get new photographs, new quotes, new stories, anything on the Prince and prospective Princess that would help to fill newspapers, magazines, and TV screens. Of course, at this stage of the game the idea was to keep raising the height of the pedestal on which to place them; it would not be until some time later that the knocking-down process would really begin. For now, there were only good things to say, the sole dissenter on the British newspaper scene being the communist *Morning Star,* which, alluding to all of the premature speculation about the kindergarten teacher becoming a mother, conceded, "surely even she deserves to be regarded with more dignity than a pedigree Frisian cow."

At the time of the engagement, Charles and Diana had given a television interview, in which she had taken her first modest steps as a small-screen celebrity in front of an estimated worldwide audience of 700 million viewers. Since then, Di had begun to acquaint herself more with posing for photographers and waving affably to crowds of onlookers, knowing very well that this would become a way of life once the events of July 29 had turned her into one of the most famous faces—if not the most famous face—in the world.

Lady Susan Hussey taught Diana how to perform the "royal wave"—a lesson in economy of movement. In order to greet the masses, the hand is capped and maneuvered in a slow, subtle circular motion at the wrist (or even a simple twitching movement) instead of frantically flapping a limp hand up and down or shaking it from side to side at the wrist. Combined with a pleasant smile and a distant gaze above ordinary citizens' heads, this adds an air of "greatness" to the performer who appears to be symbolically acknowledging "my people, my people."

Diana had displayed no such coolness and self-assurance, however, on the weekend before the wedding, when the constant barrage of press and public attention appeared to take its toll, and she openly burst into tears while watching Prince Charles playing polo at Tidworth in Wiltshire. She rose to leave, and then as the nearby Lady Romsey tried to comfort her, she broke down once again. The Prince caught sight of this and rushed over to help her to the car that would take her home. Whether this was just a simple case of premarital jitters, an outpouring of emotion after the pressures of the preceding months, or—in line with the stories that have since emerged about the couple's incompatibility—an early sign of frustration within an already troubled relationship, is all open to speculation. What is now clear, however, is that while this sort of vulnerability only endeared Diana more to the general public back in 1981, it should also have been taken as a warning sign to those around her that maybe she was not strong enough to survive the position into which she had been catapulted.

Nevertheless, on the night of July 28, while Di was going to bed early at Clarence House in preparation for a 6:30 A.M. start the next morning, Charles was visiting Hyde Park to ignite the first of 101 bonfires to coincide with the celebrations that were taking place all over the country. The estimated half-million people there, together with countless others lining the streets of the surrounding area, were then treated to a 30-minute fireworks extravaganza.

The nation's mood was electric. The festivities had begun.

Earlier that evening, around 700 million viewers across the world had seen Lady Diana Spencer's last television interview before becoming a Princess. In it she talked about how she was just becoming accustomed to her new life in the full glare of the public spotlight, and of how the prince had been "a tower of strength" during the past few months by helping her in this respect. She made the customary comments about looking forward to being a good wife and predicted that her new role would broaden her horizons, both personally and professionally. "As I'm 20, I've got a good start," she pointed out.

The proper start really took place at precisely 10:37 the next morning, when the glass coach carrying Diana and her father embarked on its journey from Clarence House to St. Paul's, pulled by the two bays, Kestrel and Lady Penelope. When they arrived at their destiny, Prince Charles and the other members of the royal family were already inside the packed cathedral, together with the heads of other royal households from Europe, Africa, and Asia. American First Lady, Nancy Reagan; Spencer family members; sports and show biz celebrities; the bride's long-time friends and acquaintances; and over 200 members of staff from Buckingham Palace, Windsor Castle,

Diana was walked down the aisle of St. Paul's Cathedral
by her father, the late Earl Spencer.

Sandringham, and Balmoral rounded out the guest list.

Those conspicuously absent included Diana's dance tutor, Miss Betty Vacani and Diana's step-grandmother, Barbara Cartland, who was evidently—and unfairly—viewed as an undesirable scene-stealer, but whose snubbing only served to gain her more attention.

Since his stroke nearly three years before, Johnnie Spencer had walked with a slight limp, but on this day he performed admirably as he accompanied his daughter up both the cathedral steps and the long aisle before arriving at the altar for the 70-minute wedding ceremony. This was conducted by the Archbishop of Canterbury, Robert Runcie, and included some notable slips of the tongue. When Diana referred to the man she was marrying as "Philip Charles Arthur George," it prompted Prince Andrew to remark that she had married his father. Charles also unwittingly substituted "And all *thy* goods with thee I share" in place of "And all *my* worldly goods with thee I share." "*That* was no mistake," observed Princess Anne.

The wedding ring placed on the bride's finger had been carved from the same nugget of Welsh gold that was used to make wedding rings for the Queen Mother, the Queen, Princess Margaret, and Princess Anne. When the Archbishop pronounced the couple man and

The wedding was performed by the Archbishop of Canterbury, Robert Runcie.

wife, a huge cheer could be heard inside the cathedral coming from the 600,000 people standing outside listening to the service over a public address system. This cheer was then echoed shortly afterward when, with the whole family standing on the balcony of Buckingham Palace, the Prince and new Princess of Wales broke with time-honored tradition and gave each other the kiss on the lips that the crowd had been calling for.

Inside the Palace, the Queen's cousin, Lord Lichfeld, had just 18 minutes in which to photograph the royal wedding portraits. To ensure that there would be no need to recall everyone for a repeat performance at a later date, he had five cameras synchronized together taking each shot. Then the 118 guests were able to sit down to a three-course meal of brill in lobster sauce, "suprême de volaille Princesse de Galles," and strawberries and cream, before Charles cut the 200-lb. hexagonal 5-foot high, 5-tiered wedding cake with his ceremonial sword.

The 10,000 wedding presents that the couple had received—more than justifying throwing such a big public wedding bash— would later go on show at St. James's Palace, raising money for charity. In the meantime, the newlyweds changed into something more comfortable, said their goodbyes, and left by carriage for Waterloo Station, performing those carefully rehearsed waves and smiles to the massed crowds that lined their route. From there they took a short train trip to Romsey, where they boarded the royal train and traveled to Broadlands for the start of the royal honeymoon. Broadlands was the Hampshire home of Lord and Lady Romsey, and the former residence of Lord Mountbatten, where Princess Elizabeth and Prince Philip had spent their wedding night in 1947.

After a couple of days spent relaxing there, during which the Prince indulged his passion for fishing, Charles then flew them to Gibraltar

where they boarded the royal yacht *Britannia* for
their Mediterranean cruise. They started out at
6:45 in the morning of August 1, to the
accompaniment of the Christopher Cross hit,
"Sailing," performed by the royal marine band.
The press had, for once, been successfully
prevented from finding out the boat's intended
destination. The photographers assembled on
the dock were even more furious when the
yacht's course and Diana's remaining below
decks ruined any ideas of capturing the fairy-
tale "lovers sailing off into the sunset" shot.

The carefully planned course saw *Britannia*
cruise off Tunis and Sardinia before moving on
to the Greek islands, where it was anchored off
Rhodes. On its way to the Red Sea, the yacht
entered the Suez Canal led by an Egyptian
minesweeper before stopping at Port Said. The
royal honeymooners spent eleven days
swimming, snorkeling, scuba diving,
sunbathing, and enjoying beach barbecues.

Three days later, Charles and Diana
returned to the United Kingdom in an RAF
VC10, touching down in Scotland where they
joined the royal family at Balmoral. During the
past two weeks the Princess had started to grow
in confidence, becoming more sexually aware
and socially relaxed aboard a yacht where the
only other woman was her dresser, Evelyn
Dagley. The honeymoon was not yet over and
married life was only beginning.

Diana and Charles publicly kissed one another on the lips on the balcony of Buckingham Palace after the wedding.

In later years, observers would note the subsequent poignancy of the Prince's reply in a television interview at the time of his engagement. When the interviewer asked Charles whether he was in love, he thoughtfully asserted "Yes, whatever that may mean."[4] There was also Di's now-enlightening refusal to utter the traditional vow that she would "obey" her husband prior to the wedding service. A lack of love, flexibility, and understanding would come to symbolize Wales' relationship before too long.

CHAPTER 7

THE PRINCE'S WIFE: LEARNING ABOUT HER HUSBANDS PAST

S hortly after they had arrived back at Balmoral, the newlyweds posed again for photographers on the banks of the River Dee, the site where royal journalist James Whitaker had first spotted the couple together just 11 months earlier. Both appeared to be in fine spirits, with Charles really looking forward to devoting some time to fishing for salmon and walking around the 24,000-acre estate.

Charles did not know how much Diana would hate daily life at Balmoral. She wanted to spend as much time as possible with her new husband learning more about his ideas and tastes. She was curious to find out what kind of

There had always been many royal functions to attend for the Prince and the Princess of Wales.

man her new husband was, and she did, but not in the way in which she had hoped for or expected. While he seemed to be perfectly content spending each day in a world of his own, waiting for fish to bite and contemplating his own thoughts, this was hardly Diana's idea of honeymoon paradise, or of married life, or of anything else for that matter. She was terribly bored!

Even aboard the yacht her new husband had often acted as if he were still a bachelor. He took a relaxing nap every afternoon and exercised every evening in the privacy of the royal bedroom. None of this had seemed to matter much at the time, but he was behaving the same way now in Scotland. Di had reason to feel that he was only happy to have her around when he so chose.

"I think Charles may have tried to spend some more time with her in the early days," said royal observer Margaret Holder, "but he was determined to keep up with his hobbies and friends from his bachelor days. Diana certainly didn't realize how set in his ways he was, or the extent to which he had enjoyed the bachelor life with the fawning courtiers and friends who made their diaries fit around him, as they still do."

The Prince, on the other hand, could not understand what all the fuss was about. Diana had never complained about being at Balmoral

Diana and Charles spent a lovely few days of their
honeymoon on the banks of the River Dee.

before, so why was she doing so now? After all,
he was simply passing his days there in the
same way he had always done, and there was
no need to have to spend every waking minute
tripping over one another. They would see each
other back at the castle later on!

After a few days of this, however, even the
Queen had noticed her daughter-in-law's
evident boredom. She encouraged her to invite
some of her friends up to stay. She did, and soon
Di was having a few more laughs in the

company of her ex-roommates and Princess Margaret's daughter, Lady Sarah Armstrong-Jones.

At the end of the three-month honeymoon, the royal newlyweds returned to London and their apartment inside Buckingham Palace. Shortly thereafter, on November 5, 1981, it was officially announced that the Princess of Wales was expecting a baby the following June. Naturally, there were plaudits from the press, public, and world leaders, but right from the start Diana had severe bouts of morning sickness. She tried to put on her best face while she undertook her initial royal duties as the Prince's wife. Just prior to the announcement of her pregnancy, she had come through her first official visit with flying colors, making a very favorable impression on the people of Wales when she and the Prince toured there from October 27 to October 29.

Diana's natural air of shy charm was just one of the qualities that those who met her during the three days fell in love with. She shook the hands of young and old, and appeared adept at the art of pleasant conversation. While horribly nervous, she gave off a feeling of serenity that put everyone at ease. Charles, meanwhile, found himself having to adapt to his new role as second fiddle, but he too looked relaxed and happy, and he seemed to accept his demotion with good grace. "I'm just a collector of flowers these days," he joked to one group of admirers.[5]

"At first, I think Diana had only been expected to fall into line with Charles," said Margaret Holder, "but then she became very, very popular and so a role had to be found for her."

In Cardiff, Di was given the Freedom of the City and gave her first public speech, partly in Welsh. "How proud I am to be Princess of such a wonderful place, and the Welsh, who are very special to me," she told the throngs of well-wishers and over 900 media people.[5]

In early December, Buckingham Palace called a meeting with national newspaper editors and television and radio producers. The Queen's Press Secretary, Michael Shea, expressed disappointment at the way in which media attention had not abated since the honeymoon. The media was requested to stick to public events and allow the royal couple to keep their private lives to themselves.

It appeared that an agreement of sorts had been reached. Yet no sooner had the dust begun to settle than certain members of the tabloid fraternity decided to get a real exclusive. In February of 1982, with Diana's pregnancy in midterm, she and the Prince decided to take a vacation in the sun instead of the usual ski trip to Klosters. Traveling on a commercial flight under the names of Mr. and Mrs. Hardy, they

The royal couple certainly seemed to enjoy each other's
company in this photo.

chose a spot where they would be far from it all
on the pencil-thin island of Windermere in the
Bahamas. Here the Princess could swim and
sunbathe wearing the briefest bikini, in the
knowledge that no one would be photographing
her swollen figure—or so she thought.

Having traced the couple there, two intrepid
photographers took it upon themselves to trek
for hours through basically jungle terrain in
order to find a vantage point. The plan was to
use their ultra high-power zoom lenses to take
the private photos that their editors had
requested. The results appeared on the front and

inside pages of two of Britain's most notorious "news" papers. The two tabloids did not consider their actions to be an invasion of privacy—after all, the island was not private property (not that it would have mattered). Buckingham Palace, however, issued a statement accusing them of "tasteless behavior." Since the papers were ecstatic with their rise in circulation, they obliged with the proper apologies.

However insincere these apologies from the press may have been, they still amounted to considerably more than either Charles or Diana were apparently prepared to give one another in the royal marriage. Diana had seemed to be far more accommodating to her husband's ideas, his interests, and his leisure pursuits before he had slipped the wedding ring on her finger. After the wedding, she seemed increasingly reluctant to follow him around as he hunted, fished, walked, and sometimes talked. Charles felt that he had been duped—she had been willing and compliant beforehand; now she was becoming a real nag and an empty-headed one at that.

He, after all, had always been a man who could come and go as he pleased, who was used to people bowing to his every whim and accepting the position that ancestry had bestowed upon him. Even in private his longest-term girlfriends had to address him as "Sir." If, like Anna "Whiplash" Wallace, they were not prepared to toe the line, then it was time to move on. Now, however, he felt trapped, for he had evidently chosen himself a very image-conscious wife, who was happy to bask in the warmth of public popularity while doing very little of consequence to assist either him or his family. It was like being married to a full-time fashion model, except that royal life amounted to more than just a fashion show.

Diana, meanwhile, was not only finding life with Charles increasingly boring, she was also frustrated. While he had made some small concessions to her requests, allowing her to update his wardrobe and so on, in the areas that concerned her most—such as love and attention—he seemed to be living on another planet. Since their engagement, she had been doing her best to remold him into the husband that she wanted, but with little real success.

Clearly, then, while Charles had misconstrued the personality of the woman whom he had decided to marry, his naive young Princess had been mistaken about him, too. She had not learned the lesson that while you can change the clothes, you cannot change the person who is wearing them.

"She did try to modernize him," confirmed Margaret Holder. "I mean, judging by the way he looked before they got married, he could have been wearing his father's clothes. He utterly missed out on the sixties and she had her work cut out over his dress sense. So he went along with that, and at the same time he also allowed for some changes to take place in the home. He had to give in, as it was a joint household, but when it came to changing his character this was almost impossible."

Worse still, Diana was also beginning to see the truth in the adage about old habits dying hard. Charles seemed to growing more cold, uncaring, and distant by the day, while she was becoming increasingly upset and disturbed by the attention that he was paying to people whom she had thought would be confined to his past.

"I don't think she knew much about him or the very long list of girlfriends," said Margaret Holder, "nor that he'd continue contact with some of them. That was a bitter blow to her."

The "them" that Holder referred to were the once-single sweethearts who became married "confidantes"—two women who shared the Prince's ideas, interests, and a lot of other things. Their enduring friendships with him did beg the question as to why he never married one of them instead. It is also, most likely, a question that the Prince of Wales continued to ask himself during the years that followed.

The first to have entered into his world was Dale Harper, whom Charles encountered when he was in Australia in 1969, prompting him to dub her with the nickname "Kanga." Through their mutual love of, among other things,

William, the first son of Diana and Charles, was born on
June 21, 1982.

hunting, fishing, and horseback-riding, they
became good friends. After she moved to
England and married, Kanga, husband
Anthony (Lord Tryon), and the Prince remained
in close touch. He would be godfather to their
second child and first son, also named Charles,
and the Tryons would be regular visitors to the
royal residences.

Much the same applied to Camilla Shand,
the niece of Lord Ashcombe, whom Charles met
when they were both in their early 20s. It
appears that the Prince did love her, but not
enough to make him want to settle down.

Camilla subsequently met and married army officer Andrew Parker-Bowles, but, as in the case of Lady Tryon, her husband did not seem to mind her continued friendship with Charles. She had the freedom to pursue their friendship, eventually qualifying as his "chief confidante."

During the early years of her marriage, however, no such generous, understanding attitude was forthcoming from Diana. After all, she was the Prince's wife, and if he had a problem or anything else that he wanted to talk about, he should be confiding in her. It also wasn't fair that he was telling other people about the intricacies of their marriage, when this was a private matter that should be sorted out between husband and wife.

From Diana's perspective, the likes of Camilla—and, to a lesser extent, Kanga—were a threat. They were likely to be telling Charles very much what he wanted to hear. He would be pouring out his troubles to them in much the same way he did with the Queen Mother when he was an unhappy schoolboy at Gordonstoun. They in turn would lend a sympathetic ear and offer like-minded advice.

Camilla had always helped check out Charles's girlfriends—including Lady Diana Spencer. This was very upsetting to Diana, since she was sure that Camilla's insights would never put her in a good light. After all, Camilla would naturally look out for herself. Diana

Charles and Diana are all smiles after his successful polo match.

needed to be on guard, since Camilla would not hesitate to put Diana down if she appeared to be getting in the way.

What must have been compounding these concerns, however, was a potent combination of anxiety and jealousy as to exactly what Charles and his confidantes were up to during all those hours that they would spend together. If the allegations that eventually came to light— courtesy of many of Diana's friends, keen observers, ex-employees of the royal households, the media—were to be believed, then the Princess had a good idea of what was going on right from the start.

If so, she probably would have hoped against hope that she was either blowing things all out of proportion in her own mind, or that things would change. As time went on, however, and the state of the marriage deteriorated, it must have become increasingly obvious neither was the case. Charles was acting with an increasing lack of concern and discretion, and Diana began to come to terms with the fact that there was no way back. What she could not yet fathom, however, was how to deal with this.

"It really is such a terrible shame," said Margaret Holder. "The royal wedding was a time of great emotional rejoicing. Britain had taken Diana to its heart. Everybody wished the royal couple well, everybody wanted to believe that fairy tale. It's very sad to see that it hasn't worked out like that."

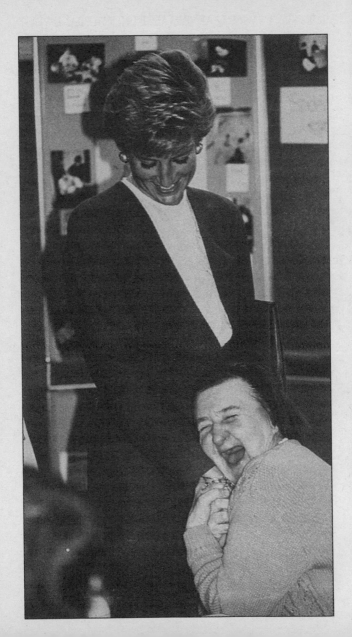

CHAPTER 8

COPING WITH LIFE, CARING FOR OTHERS

Much of Diana's life had been spent drifting. The first few years were happy enough, but then just at the age when most young children's thoughts begin to focus, her parents divorced. The security of the family home had been shattered and her whole life was thrown into chaos. The bitter power struggle at the center of the Spencer divorce left her a confused victim, and Diana's lack of academic ability had provided little hope of a vocation.

The teenage years brought further confusion and disappointment. In the best tradition of the aristocracy, little had been done by either parents or tutors in the way of mapping out a career for Diana. After all, no doubt at some

Diana's work with charities made her one of the most popular women in the world.

point in the not-too-distant future she would marry someone of her own social standing who would support and protect her while she—aided by the regulation staff of servants and nannies—would raise their children and tend to the family home.

Meanwhile, after flunking all her school tests, Di had been going around in circles and changing jobs. Conveniently, a handy cash inheritance had enabled her to buy her own home and gain some independence. When part-time work with small children appeared to be holding her interest, it seemed as if Diana's life might at last be embarking on a definite course.

Falling in love with a Prince, however, had turned her whole world upside down. All of a sudden "Shy Di" was a public figure, the face on every front page, with a world of opportunities opening up in front of her. Yet her level of ambition was still bordering on the nonexistent. By marrying and having babies she had largely achieved what she had set out to do. With everything now being done for her, the Princess could just coast along in a fairy-tale lifestyle with the perfect husband.

While fame and fortune rounded off the dream, it was marriage that Diana had envisioned as the focal point of her life. To this end, she had never been fully committed to her duties as a member of the royal family. When the romance faded and the relationship

Diana's love for children was evident in the smile she had on her face when she was around them.

crumbled, it was almost as if there was nothing left for Diana. It was certainly a terrific way of life, but there was no one to share it with.

Since shortly after her engagement to Charles in February 1981, the Princess became involved in a steady stream of charity work. As a member—or even budding member—of the royal family, it would have been just about impossible not to be involved. Apart from assignments such as meeting heads of state or attending the state opening of Parliament, almost all of her official duties were linked in one form another to a charitable cause. Were

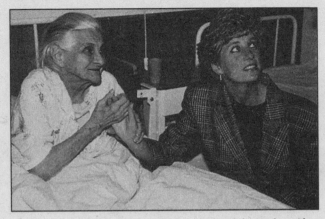

Elderly people had a special place in Diana's heart from the
time that she was in school.

this not the case, considering the modern-day
monarchy's total lack of political power, the
Crown would have a hard time trying to justify
its existence to the British taxpayers.
(Admittedly, in some quarters, it already does.)

Right from the start, Diana was personally
aligned with a number of good causes, giving
considerable support and assistance in the areas
where she felt she was most needed. But then,
when her marriage began to crumble around
her, she appeared to make a conscious decision
to throw herself more into this kind of work, to
be more conscientious, to prepare herself better,

to read assessment reports instead of just
glancing at them, and to commit herself to a
greater number and wider variety of charitable
duties. A desire to help others had always been
inside her; she decided it was time to tap into it,
giving her own life a greater sense of purpose
and achievement in the process.

One of the first organizations with which
Diana became involved was the Malcolm
Sargent Cancer Fund for Children, launched in
1968 in memory of the famous conductor who
had died from the disease. She became patron
in February 1982, and regularly attended
concerts and other functions related to the
cause. That same year she also agreed to be
patron of the Preschool Play Groups
Association. This is currently the largest single
provider of care and education for preschoolers
in England, with around 14,000 play groups
catering to 600,000 children. About £55 million
($100 million) is required each year to run these
groups. A large part of the money comes from
the parents' fund-raising efforts. Over the years
the Princess visited a number of the groups and
played with the children; she also invited
groups of them to tea parties at Kensington
Palace.

Diana's love of children, her own work both
as a nanny and as a kindergarten assistant, and
her experience of coming from a broken home,
prompted her to associate herself with a number

of infant causes during the early years of her marriage. Among the best known of these was Dr. Barnardo's, Britain's largest child-care charity, of which she was president in 1984. Subsequently, she became royal president of Dr. Barnardo's, Australia, and international president of Dr. Barnardo's, New Zealand.

After becoming president, the Princess put in many hours of work to help the organization, visiting projects and attending engagements on almost a monthly basis. In November 1985 she managed three visits in one week, and exactly two years later she upped this to three in just four days. When she was launching Dr. Barnardo's "If you let me" campaign for mentally disabled youngsters searching for jobs and places to live in 1989, she invited three such mentally challenged children to join her and a number of media representatives at Kensington Palace, where she signed the campaign charter.

Diana's charity work did not consist of lavish events, pleasant conversation, and smiling faces. Very often she came face to face with tragedy and heartache, meeting people with handicaps or terminal diseases. She actually allowed herself to become emotionally involved on a number of occasions with people on the verge of death. Distressed when learning of the deaths of people whom she met, Diana—not a secretary—often wrote to the bereaved

Diana's gentle encouragement and smile prompted even the shiest youngster to talk to her.

relatives expressing her sincere feelings of sympathy in their time of grief, as well as trying to give them some much-needed encouragement for the future.

Diana also worked in fields with heavy social stigmas attached to them, such as alcoholism, drug addiction, mental illness, AIDS, and leprosy. She became involved with various anti-narcotics campaigns during the mid-Eighties. Acknowledging the adverse effect that drugs have on society, she urged the authorities to look at ways of dealing with the causes as well as the symptoms of drug use.

Diana felt that while the difficult task of cutting the drug supply was all-important, reducing the demand would really help to eliminate the problem.

To this end, Diana became patron of the Institute for the Study of Drug Dependence, The Freshfield Service in drug counseling. She was also active in Turning Point—an organization that provides residential, day-care, and on-the-spot counseling for those suffering from mental health, alcohol, or drug-related problems. She was vocal about greater community care for those suffering from mental disorders. Her belief was that only when people were made more aware of the true nature of the problems afflicting the victims—and the fact that they could affect anyone at any time—would they be inclined to help.

One of the ways in which the Princess tried to achieve broader public recognition of these issues was by setting a well-publicized example. In March 1990, she became the first member of royalty to visit Broadmoor, the top-security prison hospital that houses many of Britain's most psychotic and violent criminals. Images of her meeting staff and inmates were flashed around the country.

In 1987, Princess Diana made headline news when she opened the AIDS unit of London's Middlesex Hospital and shook hands with patients there without wearing protective gloves. She did this again in February 1989, when visiting Europe's first AIDS hospice at Mildmays Mission Hospital in east London. During a three-day solo trip to New York later that month, she gained the respect of countless Americans when she hugged and played with seven children dying of AIDS in the pediatric unit of Harlem Hospital.

"Our own royalty, whatever that is in a republic, have not done anything nearly so symbolic as these things you are doing for us today," the hospital's director, Dr. Margaret Heagarty, told Diana. The AIDS ward's educational coordinator, Lulu King, said, "Thank you for bringing love, youth, and vitality to us here, and God bless you."[1]

Diana brought the same degree of warmth and caring to Nigeria in March 1990, when she and Charles visited a leper colony—after which she became patron of the Leprosy Mission in Britain. While on a trip to England the following year, American First Lady, Barbara Bush, got a first-hand glimpse of Diana's compassion when she too visited an AIDS ward at London's Middlesex Hospital. One of the patients started to cry while the Princess was talking to him. Diana took the man into her arms and spontaneously hugged him.

Earlier that year, Di had become patron of the National AIDS Trust. She continued to open new wards, mingle with doctors and patients, and sit in on counseling sessions. She did this because AIDS sufferers need as much help and comfort as possible, and in her eyes this was not happening.

The Princess, in fact, spent several months in 1991 helping to look after her friend, Adrian Ward-Jackson, who was dying from AIDS. He had received a CBE (Commander of the Order of the British Empire) medal at Buckingham Palace in March for his work as governor of the Royal Ballet, chairman of the Contemporary Arts Society, and director of the Theatre Museum Association. The following month his condition took a turn for the worse. The Princess was regularly at his bedside both at his home and at St. Mary's Hospital in London. When on August 19, Adrian's friend, Angela Serota, telephoned Diana in Balmoral to tell her that he only had a matter of hours to live, Diana was not able to get a flight down from Scotland. Accompanied by a detective, she drove the 600 miles and arrived at the hospital at 4 A.M. where she kept a bedside vigil for the next three days. Adrian Ward-Jackson died on August 23. While Diana was naturally saddened over his death, she had nevertheless found once again that in trying to give support to others she had discovered her own inner strength.

Diana's AIDS-related activities, however, only represent a relatively small part of her overall calendar of charitable work. She was also president of the Great Ormond Street Hospital for Children, the Royal Marsden Hospital, the General Council and Register of Osteopaths, and the National Meningitis Trust, as well as being patron to about 40 different organizations both in the United Kingdom and abroad. Her charity work dealt with a wide array of social and humanitarian problems.

Among these is RELATE, a counseling service to both married and single people who are experiencing relationship problems either in their personal life or at work. In light of her family background and her own difficulties in her marriage, Diana had a particular affinity to this organization, dedicating much of her time to it.

While attending one or two film premieres a year is a major help in raising funds for the organization, Diana's main contribution was to actually visit some of the 130 centers that RELATE has throughout the country.

In July 1991, an AIDS patient at London's Middlesex Hospital asked the Princess why her work always seemed to involve "the deaf and the sick." She replied, "Anywhere I see suffering, that is where I want to be, doing what I can."[1]

Diana was not in harmony with her husband or much of his family, but she was always prepared to abide by the Prince of Wales' motto "Ich Dien," meaning "I Serve." Diana's charity work is one of her greatest legacies.

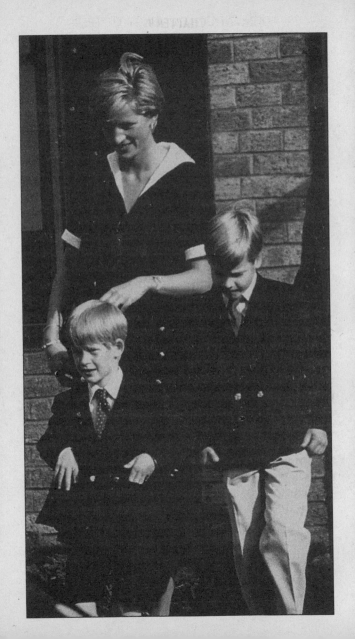

CHAPTER 9

LIFE AT COURT: THE PRIVATE PRINCESS

I f nothing else, the royal family is unique. They reside in Britain, in the western-most reaches of Europe, but in an altogether different world to the one inhabited by their fellow citizens. Theirs is a very small world, where the head of the household has her face reproduced on money and postage stamps. People stand, bow, or curtsy in her presence, and sing a song in which they ask the Lord Almighty to protect her and prolong her life. It is a world of high living, high expectations, and antiquated traditions. It is a continual stream of paperwork, protocol, and security.

This is the world into which Lady Diana Spencer walked, and to which, as Her Royal Highness the Princess of Wales, she was to become accustomed. She was barely out of her teens when she came on the scene. Even though she was a member of the aristocracy, nothing

Diana was known to be a real hands-on mom to her two sons, Harry (left) and William (right).

she had ever experienced could have possibly prepared her for this. She had never required bodyguards or people to plan her every hour of every day. (Before meeting Charles, she had never had all that much to do.) And she had never been told to mind her manners for fear of offending a nation.

Staying in London at KP—the family's term for Kensington Palace—the typical week starts off with the staff receiving typed details of Diana's forthcoming schedule, and preparing accordingly. When the Princess arose and tried to shine, her personal dresser had already readied the royal clothes and jewelry.

At around 8:30 A.M., her hairdresser arrived and, while she sat in the dressing room adjacent to the master bedroom, he set about fashioning the crowning glory of the appearance that captivated people the world over for more than a decade. Makeup was applied, and then it was time for a breakfast of grapefruit, cereal, yogurt, and Earl Grey tea with lemon.

Reflecting not only the state of their marriage but also royal tradition, Prince and Princess—when under the same roof—never ate breakfast together. Instead, each read the newspapers, opened their private mail, and then continued on their separate ways. Their day had begun.

If perhaps the Princess was going shopping at Kensington High Street, it was not usually decided on a whim. She could not "pop around the corner for an ice cream." While the shop or shops that she visited had no idea about her plans, the police headquarters at Scotland Yard and the London Ambulance Service did. When Diana drove out of the south entrance of KP with her personal bodyguard and his high-frequency radio, the police were tracking her every move by computer. When she got to her destination, an ambulance was waiting in the event she would need one.

Even when Diana was not carrying out an official engagement, but just visiting a favorite boutique or eating at her favorite restaurant, there were still about 20 people involved in the high-security operation. Just as for public functions, everything was carefully planned for the private Princess, too.

Most of Diana's friends, of course, were either rich or aristocratic—or both—but a privileged few in her social circle were sometimes even members of her staff. (This is not usually "the done thing" for the royal family. The Queen, for example, only sees her own chef on Christmas Day, when he performs the traditional lunchtime carving of the turkey!) Diana, on the other hand, was known to join the KP chef for lunch at his apartment, together with several junior officers from the Royal Protection squad. In private she allowed—and positively wanted—her friends to call her by her first name, even though they still carried out the required bows and curtsies.

Obviously the staff is there to cater to the needs of the royal couple, yet whenever one of them had personal problems due to illness or a family bereavement, Diana took it upon herself to care for them.

For all of the stories about the Princess being a fair, kind, and considerate employer, there was also much talk about the comings and goings of numerous staff members during her residence there. This led to speculation that Diana the Good could also be a "royal pain."

While Charles was intolerant of delays or inefficiency, Diana admitted that she was the perfectionist in the family. In 1985, however, she felt compelled to tell *Daily Mirror* royal correspondent James Whitaker that she was not responsible for the departure of any of her staff members. "I just don't sack people," she insisted. It did appear, though, that even if the Princess didn't fire people herself, she either ignored them until they chose to resign or she had someone else do the sacking for her.

Yet, after Charles's loyal valet, Stephen Barry, resigned soon after his master's wedding, there were rumors that he had in fact been made to leave as a result of Diana not liking the "close attention" that he had been paying to her husband. Others like Barry were to follow. The tabloids would have had us believe that

Shopping in casual dress was quite fun after spending so many days in formal attire. Jeans, a T-shirt, and a blazer seemed to do the trick for Diana.

demanding Di was a woman who was the model of kindness one minute, and then irritable the next when something was not done her way. The truth of the matter, however, was probably somewhere in between.

Such was the case, for example, with Alan Fisher, a man who had previously enjoyed the glamour and excitement of working for the likes of Bing Crosby and the Duke and Duchess of Windsor. He joined Charles and Diana as their butler in 1982. After a couple of years he left to go to the United States, explaining, "I was bored there. They never did any entertaining."[1] While taking the time to point out that he had no problems with the Prince and Princess of Wales, he described them as "the most wonderful people in the world."

Assistant private secretary Francis Cornish quit his job in 1984 to become high commissioner in Brunei, while household accountant Michael Colborne also left that year. Di's equerry, Lieutenant Commander Peter Eberle, who had been with her since 1983, left in 1986, and his short-lived replacement, Lieutenant Commander Richard Aylard, was superseded by Lieutenant Commander Patrick Jephson. The latter then replaced Anne Beckwith-Smith as Diana's assistant private secretary in 1990 and ascended to the role of private secretary the following year while the post of equerry was filled by Wing Commander David Barton.

Numerous other cooks, cleaners, chauffeurs, and housekeepers stayed a short time and left. Considerably more fuss was made about the 1985 departure of Edward Adeane, a man of solid pedigree whose family had served the royals since the reign of Queen Victoria. Since Adeane had worked happily for Charles for a couple of years before he married Diana, was it logical that she caused the split?

In fact, what really appears to have happened was that Adeane's departure was precipitated by the obstinate behavior of the Prince of Wales. The private secretary was less than happy over the years with Charles's tendency to disregard whatever advice he gave him. The Prince also significantly reduced the number of official engagements following the birth of Harry, which Adeane objected to. He was also displeased with the Wales' 1985 visit to Italy, which he felt resembled more of a sightseeing vacation than an official tour. Furthermore, it was alleged by a number of sources that Charles had intended to attend a private mass with the Pope at the Vatican. Edward Adeane was outraged that the future head of the Church of England was breaking with long-standing tradition. Adeane convened a meeting with the Catholic head of the Church of Rome, objecting strongly. Eventually, the Queen stepped in and, fearful that such a meeting would incite problems with the English Church, vetoed the whole idea. By then, however, Adeane had already quit.

The idea that Diana was the main source of discontent between the royal staff appears to have been largely a figment of the tabloid journalists' vivid imaginations.

All of this suggests that while the former Lady Diana Spencer may well have adapted to life with the royal family, she did so on her own terms. Clearly her diary was filled with official engagements six months in advance (at least it was until her whole future became unclear in 1992). Having led a normal life, making dates

Relaxing with the two pint-sized men in her life was one of
Diana's favorite pastimes.

and meeting friends whenever she wanted,
Diana became determined to carry over some of
the elements into her royal existence.

The Princess also always tried to be a proper
mother to her children, William and Harry. She
took care of them herself, rather than
constantly leaving them in the hands of a
nanny. When royal engagements took her away
from the family home, she always carried
photos of them with her and kept in constant
contact via telephone.

When William was injured after being hit
over the head with a golf club at school in June
1991, his mother was by his side as doctors at
the nearby Royal Berkshire Hospital performed

a CAT scan to assess brain damage. She was also with him in the ambulance as it sped to London's Great Ormond Street Hospital for Sick Children in order for him to undergo surgery for a depressed fracture of the skull.

At that point, Prince Charles was satisfied that all that could be done was being done. He went off to continue with his royal duties, entertaining European community officials at a performance of Puccini's opera, Tosca, at Covent Garden. He also attended an environmental conference in North Yorkshire the following day. This, of course, provided the perfect opportunity for *The Sun* to tactfully stir things up by screaming, "What kind of dad are you?" in its front-page headline.

True to her easy-going nature, Di believed in creating a relaxed, loving environment for "the heir and spare," allowing them to play and behave like normal children as much as possible. This, too, brought her into conflict with Charles. Particularly in the case of the rebellious Prince William, Charles disagreed with what he regarded as a lack of discipline.

In the early days, Diana did not want to use physical discipline as a means of curbing William's misbehavior, but in time she changed her ideas about this. "Bill the Basher," as he was known at his school, threw a few temper tantrums when he did not get his way. He tried to assert himself in the company of other children by talking about "when I am King," and referring to "grandma's castles."[4]

William and Harry appeared to be having a fairly balanced childhood. Even though their father wanted to subject them to the kind of regime that he once had been used to, Diana attempted to open their eyes and broaden their outlook beyond the narrow confines of the traditional royal upbringing. Introducing them to her friend Adrian Ward-Jackson, when he was dying from AIDS, served to show them one of life's harsh realities.

When not at school and staying at Kensington Palace, the two boys each had bedroom suites complete with kitchen, bathroom, and staff bedrooms. Built by Sir Christopher Wren and the birthplace of both Queen Victoria and Queen Mary, at that time KP served as home to four sets of royals. Charles and Di lived in Apartments 8 and 9. Prince and Princess Michael of Kent were in 10, and, just across the courtyard, Princess Margaret was in 1A. Next door to her were the Duke and Duchess of Kent.

Highgrove, on the other hand, was a different story. While Diana was much happier being in the heart of London, on certain weekends she did share Charles's preference for the quieter life. Often referred to as "Highgrave," the residence's image of genteel tranquility is flavored with the less-than-rural presence of "panic buttons" in every room, police security cameras, and infrared beams hidden behind the rose bushes.

Diana's living room overlooked the garden, its walls covered with drawings of her aristocratic ancestors and photographs of family and friends. The room reflected her love of the ballet, classical and popular music, and glass and enamel ornaments. It was her haven in which to read, write letters, listen to records, and chat on the telephone. Her London friends were rarely invited there. Highgrove was more the domain of family members and royal guests from abroad. Neighbor Camilla Parker-Bowles was a frequent visitor to Highgrove when the Princess was not around.

Diana's day usually started off with a 7 A.M. swim. With the police keeping a close eye on her, she went through her paces for about 30 minutes, before going back inside to eat her breakfast and read the newspapers. Carefully monitored activities followed. These ranged from a visit to local shops or the more distant Regency town of Bath, to playing tennis at the Hare and Hounds Hotel. In the evenings, if guests were not around, Diana would have a three-course meal, and then watch television in her study. Her husband, meanwhile, would have invariably fallen asleep from his strenuous daytime activities of hunting and gardening.

All in all then, it was just an ordinary family life.

CHAPTER 10

DIANA IN PUBLIC: THE JET-SET PRINCESS

She may be courted by the rich and famous, catered to by the top designers, and have the resources to buy the very best, yet Her Royal Majesty Queen Elizabeth II has never exactly been known as the world's snappiest dresser. Neither, for the matter, has her husband or any of her children. All have been content to follow in the long-established family tradition of donning ostentatious costumes when pageants, processions, and state occasions call upon them to do so.

The monarch and her family have chosen to maintain the carefully cultivated image of quiet dignity, rather than showbiz pizzazz so as not to distance the public on whom they depend for survival. It was foreign to them anyway . . . until Diana came along.

Diana brought a fashionable appearance to a royal family known for its staid look.

She had poise and dignity, but she also had, in her shy way, the charisma to attract all eyes toward her. At the start Lady Diana Spencer was, as she herself admitted, a little too plump for modeling high fashion outfits, and so she stuck with long skirts and high necklines. But when the public adulation came, a slimmer figure followed, and her transformation into Princess Di coincided with a growing confidence to go where no other royal had gone before. Diana would become the first Princess Superstar.

Shortly before undertaking her first public engagement with her fiancé, Lady Di was introduced by her sister, Jane, to the fashion team at *Vogue* magazine. Jane had been an editorial assistant there and knew that she was putting the budding royal in good hands. After a number of meetings in which they brought together Diana's ideas of the image that she wanted to create (glamourous yet sophisticated) and the impact that she would like to have (as much impact as possible), along with their ideas of what would suit her best, they pointed her in the direction of David and Elizabeth Emanuel for the outfit to wear for her first official outing.

The result, worn to a reception to help the Royal Opera House at Goldsmiths' Hall in London, on March 9, 1981, was a revealing black taffeta strapless dress that created the kind of effect Diana must have been hoping for. Stepping out of the limousine, Charles proudly

Every time the Princess of Wales attended a formal affair, the world watched to see what she was wearing. She rarely disappointed her fans.

told the waiting photographers, "Wait 'til you get an eyeful of this,"[2] and when his fiancée followed, the sound of the cheers of the amazed crowd was nearly matched by the sound of camera shutters.

The next morning, the national newspapers in Britain provided their readers with the same

Diana was a real hit at the White House when she chatted with First Lady Nancy Reagan in 1985.

eyeful. While certain stuffier Palace insiders were less than amused with Diana's first public exposure, this was just a hint of things to come.

Within 18 months the size 12 (U.S. size 10) Di slimmed down to a size 10 (U.S. size 8). Having whetted the public's appetite for her glamourous image, she vigorously set about buying designer clothes to meet the expectations of her adoring public. This, clearly, was a labor of love and, when she set out on her first overseas tour to Australia in 1983, she traveled with 90 trunks containing outfits by 21 different designers. "Dynasty Di" was born.

Heads of state, dignitaries, and ordinary citizens would be wowed by the clothes she wore and the way in which both her looks and her sense of originality enhanced them. She adapted Queen Mary's necklace and wore it as a headband for a dance in Melbourne, Australia, in 1985. At the America's Cup ball the following year she appeared in a Murray Arbeid gown with a black top and flame-red skirt, complemented by arm-length gloves, one red and the other black.

In both cases, the overall effect was stunning. The same would be said about Diana's choice of hats over the years.

Her wonderful new outfits needed to be offset with a subtle yet meticulously refined technique of applying cosmetics. Diana learned her tricks from her favorite make-up artist, Barbara Daly. She also picked up some handy pointers from other celebrities. Elizabeth Taylor met the Princess in 1982 when Liz was starring in the West End theater production of *The Little Foxes,* and explained to her how she gave her legendary violet eyes better definition—by applying strong eyeliner on the upper lids and brilliant blue on the inner rim of the lower ones. Di looked, listened, learned, and went for it.

"What Diana learned to do by the second half of the eighties was to simplify her style, to look smarter and more sophisticated," explained Lowri Turner. "She is tall and slim, and so she can wear things very well. That's not to say that she dresses in a particularly sexy way—she doesn't—because she has to present the classic styles. She cannot wear short skirts, for instance, and so she may leave them just above the knee. For her role she dresses very well and I therefore think Diana is a very good ambassador for British fashion."

As time wore on, the sound of applause was not exactly coming from all quarters. By the end of the eighties, the Princess of Wales had purportedly spent about $2 million on more than 750 outfits and 100 evening gowns. Furthermore, her hairstyling alone was running up a tab of around $18,000 a year.

It was a high price to pay for what was and is essentially the role of an international diplomat. During a time of economic recession and high unemployment, many Britons felt as if they were having the royal high life rubbed in their faces. After all, through their work and their very presence the members of the monarchy were supposed to be encouraging and helping the less fortunate, presenting a good image overseas, helping bridge international gaps, initiating export trade, boosting tourist revenue from abroad, and generally providing British citizens with some moral uplift during times of trouble. Wasn't this extravagance pushing things a little too far? Others asked, why not? In the meantime, little actually transpired to disrupt Princess Diana's glitzy social life.

Diana, seen here with Princess Anne, was a real trendsetter in her choice of hats.

Apart from indulging herself, however, Diana was not averse to lavishing money on others. This habit was not shared by either her husband or most other members of the royal household. They show prudence while they are still receiving a salary from the British taxpayers. At the same time, Diana's gifts of expensive clothes, jewelry, and ornaments, as well as the odd $100 box of chocolates, did result in bringing assets back into the royal coffers: Many of her friends responded in kind by presenting the Princess with equally or even more expensive art objects and items of jewelry.

You may or may not have liked the way Diana dressed, but you could never ignore her glamourous appearance. This dress, no doubt, set a fashion trend.

On December 22, 1985, Diana let her hair down at a Christmas party show for supporters of the Royal Ballet and Opera at the Royal Opera House in Covent Garden. Having settled down in a box to watch the gala with Prince

Charles and some friends, Diana then sneaked out and to everyone's astonishment (including Charles), walked on stage to roars of approval from the audience. The cheers and sense of amazement subsequently doubled when she joined dancer Wayne Sleep in a three minute performance, dancing to the Billy Joel hit "Uptown Girl." The Princess had chosen this song, and Sleep had choreographed and rehearsed with her in secret at Kensington Palace. This was intended as a pre-Christmas surprise for Charles; it certainly must have taken his breath away.

The previous month Diana had also been called upon to show off her dancing prowess, when she and Charles attended a White House banquet thrown by President Reagan and wife Nancy in the royal couple's honor during a five-day trip to Washington, D.C., and Palm Beach, Florida. Given the glamourous image of the guests of honor as well as the connections of the hosts, this was, needless to say, a star-studded affair.

In attendance that night to see the Princess in her blue off-the-shoulder Victor Edelstein gown were the likes of Clint Eastwood, Neil Diamond, Tom Selleck, Mikhail Baryshnikov, and John Travolta. Clint, Neil, Tom, and the fun-loving President all attempted to display their talents by dancing with Diana. Later the floor cleared as everyone gathered to watch the

Princess put through her paces by Travolta as they danced to the accompaniment of "You're the One That I Want," one of the actor's popular songs from his 1978 movie smash, *Grease.*

Other highlights of the White House ball included musical performances by Neil Diamond, opera star Leontyne Price, and Nancy Reagan, who charmed the guests with her tear-jerking rendition of "I Concentrate On You." The President, however, stole the show. When speaking at the table of honor, he made the simple mistake of referring to Diana as "Princess David."[1]

This was the positive side to Diana's very public image. It was easy to see Diana as an attractive, warm, witty, charming, and vivacious young woman. It is comforting to think of her as a person who spread light and happiness, put people at ease, was a welcome complement to her slightly more reserved husband, and represented her country in the best possible way.

After a while, though, Diana made a concerted effort to place more emphasis on the caring side of her nature through her official work. She downplayed the public displays of glitz, glamour, and frivolous public behavior, in order to try to dispel the jet-set superstar persona.

While the image moderated, the high spending continued. Between her health, beauty, and fashion needs, and the generosity displayed toward friends, she managed to find her way through close to half a million dollars a year. On the flip side, she became president or patron of about 70 different organizations. During the years 1987–1991 she was outdone only by Princess Anne, the Queen, and the Duke of Edinburgh, in her total of 2,247 public engagements carried out at home and abroad.[1]

Diana was unique both in terms of her image and the media scrutiny that she was constantly, incessantly subjected to. No other Princess in history, not even Princess Grace of Monaco, experienced this. Commenting on the fact that Diana had begun to be photographed wearing jeans, sweaters, and baseball caps, playing down the cover girl image and stressing that she is just an ordinary mother, Lowri Turner was asked if this was due to Diana's newfound confidence in her role. Turner responded by saying, "Either that, or she's just stopped caring."

UNSURE PROSPECTS: TRUTH OR DARE

On June 12, 1992, the Queen and Prince Charles met at Buckingham Palace for a crisis conference. The immediate cause for their concern was Andrew Morton's book, *Diana: Her True Story,* which was also serialized in the London *Sunday Times.* Over the years there had been rumors about the state of the Prince's marriage to the Princess of Wales, but this time they were afraid that the writing was truly on the wall. The publicity generated by this book had put the whole future of the royal family in danger.

The Prince and his mother were faced with the unenviable task of damage control. Somehow they needed to give the impression that life at the palace was not so bad, or else public opinion would really swing against the two of them.

Even a Princess needed to spend some time alone to think about her life.

Having been described as a cold, uncaring, unfaithful husband and father who placed royal duties above concern for his wife and children, Charles was now faced with three options. He could pretend that Diana had absolutely nothing to do with the Morton book and that the marriage was perfectly fine; he could immerse himself in work and try to boost his image to get public sympathy; or he could fight back and tell his own side of the story.

While none of these choices were guaranteed to achieve the desired effect, the first one was, quite simply, out of the question. Pretending that nothing had happened would certainly result in public condemnation for the heir to the throne and his relatives. Options two and three, on the other hand, could precipitate constitutional problems.

While a successful public relations campaign could serve to boost his image as a thoughtful, caring, hard-working Prince—a "man of the people"—the disintegration of his marriage could have prohibited him from ever becoming King Charles III. Having his friends attack Diana in the same way that hers had attacked him would almost certainly finish off the marriage and with it his hopes of ascending to the throne.

With permission from the Queen—in negotiation with the prime minister or the privy council—he could remarry, but that scenario

Queen Elizabeth II tried to come up with a solution to
Charles and Diana's problems.

creates other complications. Since the sovereign
is the supreme governor of the Church of
England (which does not approve of divorce), it
would be difficult for the Queen to give this kind
of assent. Also it would be almost impossible for
a divorced heir to succeed her as the head of the
Anglican Church. The only divorced person who

has ever succeeded the British throne was George I, and that was almost 300 years ago.

It was a very difficult situation, mother and son concurred during their June 12 meeting, particularly since Prince Philip, the chief decision-maker in the royal household, was away. On June 15, after the annual Order of the Garter ceremony, the three of them met behind closed doors at Windsor Castle. This time, the Princess of Wales was present, too. It was after this conference that word leaked out that divorce had been rejected. In its place was a suggested six-month cooling-off period during which the couple would attempt to put on a united front in public. Some time was bought, but a solution still needed to be found to patch up Charles's bruised and battered image.

The following week a third meeting was convened between the Prince and his advisers. They came up with a four-point plan that was a compromise between all three options: 1. A public relations campaign coordinated by aides at both Buckingham and Kensington Palaces would focus on Charles's devotion to his work, his country, and the environment. 2. It would be made known that the Prince's friends were privately fuming about all of the unfair allegations about him, but, having been requested by him to retain a dignified silence for the sake of the children, they would not air their grievances in public. 3. After some time,

Charles's friends would make their anger and frustration public, recounting his side of the story to the media. This would all be done anonymously, since Charles, being such a paragon of virtue, would be terribly upset to find out that his friends went against his wishes—even if to save his image. 4. All of the marital problems would be attributed to Diana, but—and this was central to the whole plan— she would not be held accountable. After all, she had been suffering from bulimia since before the marriage, prompting severe depressions and unreasonable behavior. Her refusal to be treated had only exacerbated these problems.

This was the perfect plan. It was a way of admitting that there had been difficulties in the marriage of the Prince and Princess of Wales, but that Charles had not been responsible and Diana could hardly be blamed. Andrew Morton's book was slanted by Di's misguided outlook, brought on by her ongoing struggle with bulimia nervosa. If she would agree to be treated, then the situation might be resolved!

Parts one, two, and three of the plan were simultaneously put into operation on June 28, 1992, when a full-page article appeared in the *Sunday Times* under the heading, "The Case for Charles." To endear the readers to him, the article was supplemented by a large photograph showing an amenable-looking Prince shaking hands with members of the public. The piece reported on the three behind-the-scenes crisis meetings, the decision for him to immerse himself more in his work, and the comments of some who thought that, given the Prince's valuable contribution to issues such as architecture and the environment, this would be an excellent way of boosting his image.

The article then proceeded to name a number of Charles's sympathizers who had spoken to journalists, Neil Mackwood and Tim Rayment, but refused to be quoted for the record. Among these were the ex-King Constantine of Greece; the Prince's cousin, Lord Romsey and his wife, Patricia, Countess Mountbatten of Burma; confidante Candida Lycett-Green; and hunting companion Didi Saunders. There were, however, a number of anonymous quotes by "friends" and "family members," all admitting that the royal marriage was in ruins, but insisting that the Prince represented in the Morton book was not the man they knew. Some of Charles's sympathizers also retold some of the stories that had appeared in *Diana: Her True Story* in a different light. One informant went so far as to say, "Charles has told me that divorce is not out of the court as it was, say, one year ago."

The final part of the initial four-point damage control plan was put into effect on

Monday, July 6, when a series entitled "Charles: His True Story" began running in the U.K.'s *Today*. "Specially researched and prepared" by one of the Prince's biographers, Penny Junor, the articles used the accounts of more anonymous campaigners in the pro-Charles camp, who expressed their anger at the way in which the couple's "most private secrets" had been revealed in a conspiracy against him. They also pointed out, however, that it was the onset of Diana's bulimia, brought about by an unhappy childhood, that had caused problems "before the first night of marriage."

Junor stated that Charles's friends had asked her to write the article in order to set the record straight. She explained that periodically throughout the marriage the Princess had been mentally unbalanced because of her bulimia, and it was her illness that caused her to distort the truth and use her husband as a scapegoat. The writer then went on to assert that Charles adored his sons, but that his attempts to be with them had been thwarted by Diana. When he tried to help her, he was met with "tears and shouting." Camilla Parker-Bowles had helped the Prince to "maintain his sanity in a traumatic marriage." They were close, but nothing more than just "very good friends."

These points were made by Junor on national television and radio at the same time

Above all else, the royal duty of this couple was to appear united for the masses.

as people were reading them in *Today*. She concluded that, in her view, it would take a miracle for the marriage to survive, since too much damage had already been done. On the other hand, she claimed that if Diana—whose bulimia had been under control for the past month—would agree to have treatment for her illness, then Charles might be prepared to give their relationship another go.

"There's no soap opera I know of which could compare to the bizarre situation that the House of Windsor is in now," said royal observer, Margaret Holder. "Not even *Dynasty* at its height. Every day some other facet is appearing. Even the most hardened watchers are stunned by what is going on.

"It may not be as bad as the days of George III, when there were some shocking characters on the scene, but in a modern democracy royal behavior has to be seen as acceptable, because they are being paid by the taxpayers. So the royals are going to have to adapt, or there will be such public outcry that Parliament will have to act, though it probably won't happen during the reign of this Queen. The big question is whether Charles is fit to become King. If he did, I don't believe any government of the day would get on with him."

And so, Diana's future was decided in private, discussed in public, and handed to her on the proverbial silver platter. She was expected to put up a good front, adapt as commissioned, and to accept the awful situation in which she found herself. She (and Charles) would lead separate personal lives, but join forces in raising their children.

CHAPTER 12

DIANA SOLO: A NEW START

If, in the summer of 1992, either Charles or Diana harbored any serious hopes of saving their marriage, these were soon dashed by a series of new uproars.

The first of these, revealed by *The Sun* in August of that year, was based on a New Year's Eve, 1989, telephone call between Diana and a certain James Gilbey. Talking on his car phone, Gilbey repeatedly addressed Diana as "Squidgy" and "darling"—according to the transcript that was reproduced in the tabloid newspaper. "Oh Squidgy, I love you, I love you," he pledged at one point, to which "Squidgy" responded, "You are the nicest person in the whole wide world." Hardly a full-scale admission of a physical relationship, but tantalizing nevertheless.

For Diana and Charles, it seemed to be time to go their separate ways.

Perhaps most damning, however, was the part in which "Squidgy" referred to her royal relatives with a number of expletives. Said family was not amused.

At this point Diana reportedly considered packing her bags and walking out on the marriage, yet by October 1992, Palace officials were trying to persuade anyone who would listen that Charles and Diana had somehow managed to iron out their differences. Perhaps there was a genuine if tenuous hope that the couple could reconcile. Whatever the truth, the hope did not last long.

On November 14, Charles spent his 44th birthday at Highgrove while Diana was away in France. A short time later British Prime Minister John Major read a Buckingham Palace statement to the House of Commons, announcing that the couple were separating, but not divorcing. They would live apart and carry out their royal duties on separate schedules.

However, fast on the heels of "Squidgygate," came "Camillagate." *The Daily Mirror* reported on a tape of yet another phone conversation, also dating back to December 1989, but this time involving Charles and Mrs. Camilla Parker-Bowles.

If the transcript, revealed in January 1993, had only amounted to lines such as Charles cooing, "I adore you. I am so proud of you,"

Confidante to Charles, Mrs. Camilla Parker-Bowles.

and Camilla responding, "I love you, darling," it would have been no match for the "Squidgy" tape. However, there was more, much more, to stir the public interest.

A brief sampling would include statements such as Camilla telling Charles, "You're awfully good at feeling your way along," to which Charles retorts, "Oh stop! I want to feel my . . . up and down you and in and out . . . particularly in and out." In this same poetic, love-struck mood, Charles, the future King, also talks about needing Camilla "several times a week," and wanting to live in her trousers. The rest of the conversation included his now-famous "tampon" reference.

With tapes of Charles and Diana confiding in their respective "confidantes," there only needed to be one of the Prince and Princess actually conversing with each other in order to complete the set. It wasn't long in coming. In May 1993 *The Sun* obliged with a transcript of yet another tape, although this one wasn't taken from the phone but actually inside Highgrove, and the dialogue that Charles and Di were indulging in wasn't exactly love talk. In fact they were feuding just prior to their separation the previous year.

If ever the game was up it was now. It was hard for the Palace to even take a stab at any more damage limitation, but it tried . . . on behalf of Charles. Clearly, Diana was a long lost cause, and so there was now a concerted effort to slowly rehabilitate the image of the future monarch by not-so-gently ousting his estranged wife from the picture. On December 3, 1993, close to tears while standing before 500 guests at a charity gathering at the Park Lane Hilton in London, she announced her retirement from public life.

"I hope you can find it in your hearts to understand and to give me time and space that has been lacking in recent years," Diana stated. Recent intense media attention had been "hard to bear," and so she now hoped to focus her efforts on a few charitable causes and find a "way of combining a meaningful public role with, hopefully, a more private life." Indeed, Diana's most important mission would now be to devote herself to bringing up 11-year-old William and 9-year-old Harry, who "deserve as much love, care and attention" as she could give them.

Amid talk of this and the Princess even having to leave Kensington Palace, there was a backlash against Charles in the British press. After he'd gone fox hunting, one Sunday paper carried the front-page headline, "He broke Diana's heart. Twenty-four hours later he went out for a bit of fun . . . killing animals."

The Mail on Sunday published an opinion poll in which 31 percent of the British public asserted that they would like to see Prince William succeed the Queen on the throne.

Prince Charles and his advisers were not prepared for this kind of reaction, and the casting of him as the villain and Di as the victim would continue throughout what had been intended as his "comeback year" of 1994.

Not that life was getting any easier for her either.

There undoubtedly had been cause for Diana to cite her need for greater privacy during her "retirement" speech at the Hilton. Just a few weeks earlier, on November 7, photos of her exercising at London's LA Fitness Center health club had been published in The *Sunday Mirror* along with the headline "Di Spy Sensation." More photos appeared in *The Daily Mirror* during the next couple of days, and it was revealed that the "spy" who had taken them with a hidden camera was Bryce Taylor, the owner of the health club, who had sold his snaps for a tidy £100,000 ($150,000).

Diana sued Bryce Taylor and in July 1994, she would agree to an out-of-court settlement. In the meantime, if she felt betrayed by the owner of her fitness club, this was nothing compared to the treachery of riding instructor James Hewitt. In March 1994, he made £100,000 by selling his story of their liaison to *The Daily Express,* describing how he'd found the Princess to be "attractive" and how she had once collapsed in his arms, sobbing about her unhappy marriage. The implication was they were just good friends, yet it amounted to a lot more than that in October, when *Princess in Love* appeared in the bookstores.

Written by Anna Pasternak, but based entirely on Hewitt's account, it told the story of his and Di's five-year affair, which began in 1986, and resulted in the Captain sleeping over at Kensington Palace whenever Charles was away. The book's publisher claimed that Hewitt made nothing from the kiss-and-tell biography, but the British tabloids asserted that he'd earned several million pounds. A couple of years later this cache would be supplemented by the airing on American TV of the quickie movie *Princess in Love.*

As for the Prince of Wales, in June 1994, ITV aired a 2½-hour documentary entitled *Charles: The Private Man, The Public Role,* in which, among many other things, he admitted to interviewer David Dimbleby that he had indeed embarked on an affair with Camilla Parker-Bowles while he was still married. This, however, was only after the marriage "became irretrievably broken down." Few people bought into that line of justification, and the following day's newspapers were full of photos . . . of Diana, arriving at a London arts gala decked out in a low-cut, shoulderless, wraparound Valentino dress.

Once again the Princess had managed to upstage her increasingly frustrated husband. In Jonathan Dimbleby's book, *Prince of Wales: A Biography,* Charles confessed that he had never loved Diana but that he had been pressured into marrying her by Prince Philip. This was not good public relations either.

If 1994 proved to be a bad year for Charles, it was Diana's turn to take the hits in 1995. That March, a month after she had visited New York amid rumors that she might move there permanently, her former chauffeur, Barry Hodge, sold his story to the tabloid papers. He alleged that Diana was involved in an ongoing affair with a married art dealer named Oliver Hoare. This was hardly a revelation to royal insiders and observers, for the previous year it had been "mentioned" repeatedly that Di had been "pestering" Hoare by making countless anonymous nuisance phone calls to his home. He and his wife were now in the midst of divorce. Diana's image was further tarnished that August when the wife of England's rugby captain alleged that the Princess was openly flirting with her husband, Will Carling. Matters weren't helped when the Carlings split up the following month. In November, on Charles' 47th birthday, Diana's gift to him was the announcement that she had recorded an interview for BBC TV's *Panorama* program. However it came about, neither Charles, his mother, nor Palace officials knew anything about this, and when the 55-minute show aired in Britain before an estimated audience of 21.5 million people, their worst fears were realized.

Talking to *Panorama*'s Martin Bashir, Diana discussed a relationship with Charles, that she had "desperately wanted to work," before coming to the realization that "There were three of us in this marriage, so it was a bit crowded." Admitting to her own affair with Captain James Hewitt, who she'd "adored" and had been "in love" with, Diana opined that, while she didn't expect to become Queen of England, Charles didn't even want to become its King.

Stressing that she had no desire to divorce Charles, Diana vowed to "fight to the end, because I believe I have a role to fulfill and I have two children to bring up." If Charles wanted a divorce he would have to initiate it. Advantage Di. *The Daily Mail* asserted that the interview now "plunged the monarchy into the greatest crisis since the abdication [of Edward VIII]," yet the official response from the Palace was a conciliatory offer to "meet with the Princess to see how we can help her define her future and continue to support her."

Privately, of course, the Queen was outraged. On December 17, 1995, she sent letters to her eldest son and his wife expressing her "anger and frustration" at the way in which they had aired their dirty laundry in public, and urging that "an early divorce is desirable." We know what the Queen wrote because three days later the letter was "leaked" to the media, apparently with the Queen's approval. Diana was unprepared for this, but it was now the Monarch's turn to show her strength. For one thing, she had the constitutional right to supervise the upbringing of the potential heirs to the throne if she so chose. For another, this latest move also prevented Charles from being the one to have to press for a divorce and therefore be cast as the villain once again. Advantage the Queen.

Not too surprisingly, Diana decided to opt out of that year's family Christmas party and therefore stayed at Kensington Palace without her sons. Then it emerged that, at the royal staff Christmas party on December 14, there had occurred what the press referred to as "The Seven Words War" between Di and the boys' nanny, Alexandra "Tiggy" Legge-Bourke. Thought to be based upon Diana's jealousy and overactive imaginings, this episode only served to confirm a general feeling within royal circles that Diana was suffering from extreme paranoia. Her private secretary resigned soon afterward, followed by his assistant and the chauffeur.

On February 28, 1996, just over an hour and a half after a meeting with Charles, Diana announced through her press secretary, Jane Atkinson, that she had agreed to a divorce and would be maintaining her title. Taken totally by surprise, the Palace responded that all such matters "remain to be discussed and settled." For his part, Charles apparently "blew his top."

Meanwhile, all of this divorce talk had the press speculating about a settlement, given that

Di's estimated annual expenses—excluding accommodations—was about $245,000. In the end, August saw a lump-sum payoff of around $26 million. Diana would continue to live at Kensington Palace and to share responsibility for the raising of the children, yet she would be stripped of the title Her Royal Highness and now simply be addressed as Diana, Princess of Wales. Charles had already informed 40 of her favorite stores that all future bills should be sent directly to her—even the royal charge card had been taken away!

No longer an official member of the Royal Family, Diana now set about redefining her role and her public image. She had already dispensed with her personal bodyguards—a move that was widely criticized when she was involved in a five-car pileup in London in 1996—and then, in mid-January 1997, she embarked on a four-day trip to war-torn Angola. This was in support of an international Red Cross campaign to ban land mines that were killing and maiming innocent civilians.

Di would visit Bosnia as part of the same campaign, while, on June 25, and at Prince William's suggestion, she had 79 of her dresses auctioned off at Christie's in New York. These fetched $3.26 million, which she donated to AIDS and cancer charities, along with another $2.5 million, which was raised by catalog sales and tickets to the previews.

A pictorial and interview in the July issue of *Vanity Fair* (published in June) had helped publicize the dress auction, while also providing the public with images of a blonde, straight-haired, youthful-looking Princess. Her star appeared to be firmly on the rise. While confronting a photographer named Brendan Beirne outside a gym in London's Earl's Court on Easter Monday, Di had been assisted by a passer-by who proceeded to place Beirne in an arm-lock while she ripped the film from his camera. Now, in July, while she and the children were houseguests at the St. Tropez home of Egyptian-born plutocrat Mohammed Al Fayed, the photographers were on the prowl once again.

Al Fayed, the owner of London's Harrods department store, is well known in the UK for his unsuccessful attempts to become a British citizen, for the part that he played in bringing down the Conservative Government by revealing that he had paid some Tory Members of Parliament cash to ask questions in the House of Commons. It was his eldest son, Dodi, who Princess Di was actually interested in.

The couple first met in 1986, when Dodi's polo team had beaten one led by Charles. A 42-year-old playboy with a reputation for liking fast cars, beautiful women, and not paying his bills, he had enjoyed a patchy career in Hollywood. In reality, he had co-produced and co-financed such successful films as *Chariots of Fire, The World According to Garp,* and *Hook.* Now, apparently, he and Diana were besotted with each other (to the extent that he had broken off his engagement to model Kelly Fisher, in return for which she would attempt sue him for breach of contract).

The paparazzi were having a field day. There were shots of the couple looking smitten in St. Tropez, Paris, and, most notably, off the coast of Sardinia. While on board Mohammed Al Fayed's $32-million yacht, extra-powerful telephoto lenses fuzzily captured them locked in an embrace.

In Britain there was also a feeling in some circles that the Al Fayed's were trying to gain respectability by way of their association with the Princess of Wales, and that she in turn was thumbing her nose at the British establishment by keeping company with this notorious family. In fact, in August, Diana granted an interview to a French newspaper in which she asserted that, due to all of the pressure, she would have left Britain long ago if it hadn't been for the fact that her sons had to remain there.

Clearly, this was a woman in transition. Still, the big question remained to be answered: Was the relationship with Dodi Al Fayed leading to marriage, or was this just a summer romance?

CHAPTER 13

A TRAGIC END: DEATH IN PARIS

Having jetted their way to Paris on the afternoon of Saturday, August 30, 1997, Princess Diana and Dodi Al Fayed settled into their $2,000-a-night suite at the Ritz Hotel, yet another of the properties owned by Dodi's father. Local photographers waited outside the hotel's entrance, but Dodi's chauffeur drove off in a Range Rover in order to distract the assembled paparazzi.

That evening, in a telephone conversation with the *Daily Mail*'s Richard Kay, Diana said that she was planning to gradually wind down her charity work in order to dedicate more time to personal affairs. Kay would later assert that she was "as happy as I have ever known her. For the first time in years all was well with her world."

One of many memorials to Diana,
Princess of Wales.

There certainly didn't appear to be very much that was wrong. Diana's relationship with Charles and her former in-laws was progressing on a more even keel, she was enjoying an active role in the raising of Princes William and Harry, and she had found jet-set romance and excitement in the form of wealthy Dodi Al Fayed.

Around 10:30 in the evening Di and Dodi ate dinner in the Ritz's L'Espadon restaurant. Less than hour later, the maitre d'hotel informed them that 30 or so photographers were waiting outside, the couple returned to their suite and planned their getaway. They would head for Dodi's apartment nearby. At around 11:45, his chauffeur once again climbed into the Range Rover and sped away in order to serve as a decoy to the photographers. The ruse didn't appear to work.

At 12:20 A.M., fed up with waiting, the Princess and her beau got into the hotel's armor-plated Mercedes S 280. The photographers immediately went to work, taking— although no one could have realized it at the time—some of the last photos of the duo. They weren't the very last, though; as we soon found out.

Driving the car was former French Air Force commando, Henri Paul, the Ritz's assistant director of security. He had twice completed a Mercedes-Benz training course. At 7:30 that evening he'd gone off duty, returning (as witnessed by the hotel's time—coded surveillance video) at 10:10. Soon he would fill in for Dodi's regular chauffeur, but what Al Fayed possibly didn't realize was that, during the intervening hours, Henri Paul had been consuming alcohol—it would later be disclosed that his blood alcohol level was between three to four times the French legal limit, or roughly equivalent to about ten glasses of wine.

Knowing that some of the photographers were preparing to give chase on their motorcycles, Paul screeched away. Sitting next to him in the front passenger seat was Al Fayed's Welsh bodyguard, Trevor Rees-Jones. Di and Dodi were together in the rear. The car sped onto an expressway running alongside the River Seine with the bike-riding photographers in close pursuit. According to some of their later recollections, it was after stopping at a red light that the car really pulled away at a tremendous speed, hurtling into a narrow tunnel not far from the Eiffel Tower at a speed variously estimated at up to 120 miles per hour. It was now 12.35 A.M. With the motorbikes a few hundred yards behind, the Mercedes veered out of control at a slight curve in the road, hit the tunnel's thirteenth concrete support column, spun around and slammed into the facing wall.

The front of the car was unrecognizable, the famed Mercedes radiator grille having been pushed virtually into the front seats, while the roof was crushed, the windshield smashed and the air-bags deployed. Henri Paul, slumped, over the wheel so that the horn blared inside the tunnel, was dead. So was Dodi Al Fayed. The paparazzi arrived on the scene within seconds and one of the photographers used his cellular phone to call the emergency services. As things turned out, it would take the ambulances about 15 minutes to arrive, during which time—according to eyewitnesses—some of the photographers began pressing their camera lenses up against the car windows in order to capture the bleeding, moaning, semi-conscious blonde woman laying on the back seat.

According to some witnesses, when the police arrived certain photographers pushed them out of the way in order to get a few more priceless snapshots. If this is true, *these* were probably the last photos of Diana. Seven photographers were immediately arrested, facing charges of involuntary manslaughter and failing to aid accident victims, and their precious film was confiscated. Others evidently got away.

Within a couple of days crash-scene photos would be published in a German magazine. It took emergency crews more than an hour to extricate Diana and Trevor Rees-Jones, both seated on the right-hand side, from the armor-plated wreckage, and at around 2:00 A.M. they were rushed to one of Paris's best hospitals, La Pitie-Salpetriere. Rees-Jones, the only one of the four passengers to have been wearing a seat belt, was very badly injured but expected to live.

Diana's condition, on the other hand, was a different story.

Early news broadcasts suggested that the Princess had a concussion, a lacerated thigh, and a broken arm. The truth, however, was far worse. Having also sustained severe head injuries and a major blow to her left lung, upon arriving at the hospital Diana quickly went into cardiac arrest as the result of profuse bleeding into her chest cavity. Surgeons performed an urgent thoracotomy (opening the chest) and discovered a serious wound to the left pulmonary vein that carries blood from the lungs to the heart. This was sealed, yet, despite concerted efforts to restart Diana's circulation by repeatedly massaging her heart both internally and externally, the doctors finally had to admit defeat. At 4:00 A.M. local time on Sunday, August 31, 1997, Diana was pronounced dead. French Interior Minister, Jean-Pierre Chevenement, made the official announcement. "She was a woman who was modern, courageous and sensitive to human distress," he said. "Her death will be felt with great pain in our country." This was only the beginning of the tributes.

In Britain, where most people woke up to the almost unbelievable news, Prime Minister Tony Blair was close to tears when stating that he was "utterly devastated. We are today a nation in a state of shock, in mourning, in grief that is so deeply painful for us," he said.

On that last day of August, while Prince Charles—on a family vacation in Balmoral—had to inform his two sons that their mother was dead. World leaders such as Bill Clinton, Boris Yeltsin, and Nelson Mandela began to offer their own eulogies, and while Charles flew to Paris with Diana's two sisters in order to return the Princess's body back to the UK, people everywhere appeared to suffer a personal and collective loss.

The scenes of mass grieving included people gathering outside Buckingham Palace, Kensington Palace, and British Embassies around the globe. In the ensuing days, even those images were superseded by the unprecedented number of floral tributes and handwritten messages that were personally delivered to Buckingham and Kensington Palaces, and numerous British embassies and consulates around the world. By Wednesday, September 3, there were 43 condolence books that had been signed by the incessant stream of mourners at St. James' Palace in London, where Diana's body lay unseen by the public. Similar condolence books drew similar crowds at the aforementioned embassies and consulates.

One aspect of the public reaction was peace and calm. Another, however, was unbridled anger; anger not only at the paparazzi, who, it was continually reported, had virtually chased the Princess to her death, but also at the news media in general—at the publishers who are prepared to shell out vast sums of money for intrusive photos, at the editors who choose to run these photos alongside scandalous articles, and at those individuals who elect to buy the journals in which these items appear. In other words, people were even angry at themselves.

"I always believed the press would kill her in the end," asserted Diana's brother, Charles Spencer, "yet not even I could imagine that they would take such a direct hand in her death, as seems to be the case . . . It would appear that every proprietor and editor of every publication that has paid for intrusive and exploitative photographs of her, encouraging greedy and ruthless individuals to risk everything in pursuit of Diana's image, has blood on his hands today."

In Britain, much of the public's anger was reserved for an altogether different faction—the royal family. After all, hadn't these been the mean, uncaring people who had treated poor Diana in such a terrible way? And hadn't Charles been the unloving husband who had reluctantly entered into marriage with a mistress at the ready? Many people were placing the blame squarely on the shoulders of the Windsors for the events leading up to Diana's death.

They were also less than happy with the Palace's announcement that, instead of a state funeral, Diana would be accorded a "unique funeral for a unique person." Then there was the family's conspicuous lack of public grieving, or, for that matter, of any proclamation of affection for Diana; it had simply issued a three-line communiqué, thanking the people for their affection.

In fact, what was being overlooked was that there are rarely—if ever—any public displays of emotion. As for the question of a state funeral, this is only reserved for members of the royal family—which Diana no longer was—or for notable leaders.

Still, Diana's "unique funeral" was clearly arranged as a concession to public demand, not to mention the subtle but steady pressure applied by Prime Minister Tony Blair, who had described her as "the people's princess." Sensing that people's patience was running out and that it was involved in a fight for its own survival, the Monarchy announced that the Union Jack would fly at half-mast over Buckingham Palace on the day of the funeral; and the funeral route itself, originally limited to one mile through the center of London, was extended to three.

For some, this was too little, too late. "Not one word has come from a royal lip, not one tear has been shed in public from a royal eye," complained *The Sun*. "It is as if no one in the royal family has a soul. From the outside looking in, the House of Windsor seems a cold, compassion-free zone where duty and protocol push emotions into a dark corner."

In London, Princes Andrew and Edward walked through the streets and acknowledged the crowds en route to looking at the vast ocean of tributes outside Buckingham Palace. The next day, the Queen, Prince Philip, and Princes Charles, William, and Harry met with the public outside Kensington Palace.

The headlines continued to display new and revised allegations regarding the accident. It was almost impossible to separate fact from rumor regarding Henri Paul's blood alcohol level, the speed at which the black Mercedes had been traveling, and the timing and positioning of the motorbikes of the impugned paparazzi.

Some of the UK headlines addressed the royals. "Your people are suffering," screamed a front-page banner headline in *The Daily Mirror*. "Speak to us Ma'am." And so she did, in an unprecedented *live* broadcast to the nation (also televised around the world) at 6 o'clock British time on the evening of September 5.

Talking to the nation in her capacity as the Monarch "and as a grandmother," the Queen paid tribute to "an exceptional and gifted human being," who she "admired and respected." William and Harry would be properly cared for she assured her subjects, recommending they all "thank God for someone who made many, many people happy." Diana, Queen of Hearts, who had privately and publicly supported so many, was finally being acknowledged by the Queen.

That night, with masses of people looking

on, Princess Diana's coffin was transported from St. James' Palace to Kensington Palace in preparation for the "unique funeral." An estimated 2.1 billion viewers tuned in around the world to see London's biggest crowd since the end of World War II on the procession route. But for the occasional sounds of crying or shouts of "We love you, Diana," there was relative silence as the horse-drawn cortege made its way toward Westminster Abbey, through Wellington Arch, normally reserved for sovereigns. This was just one of many more remarkable concessions made by the royal family on this unforgettable day.

The Queen, Princess Margaret, Princess Anne, Prince Andrew, and Prince Edward all stood outside Buckingham Palace waiting for the cortege. The Queen bowed as Diana's coffin passed by. Further along the route, the Princes Philip, William, Harry, and Charles walked behind the coffin alongside Earl Spencer. This would be an occasion to remember.

The 2,000-strong congregation at Westminster Abbey largely comprised Diana's family, friends, and associates, rather than the usual array of dignitaries and world leaders. Among them numerous celebrities and people from charitable organizations, yet notable for their absence were the editors of Britain's tabloids. They had been invited, only to be uninvited by Earl Charles Spencer.

The service contained readings by Diana's sisters and Prime Minister Tony Blair, yet there was no eulogy. One of the highlights was a special rendition of "Candle In the Wind" by Elton John. This song, originally composed as a tribute to Marilyn Monroe, now had new lyrics—courtesy of Bernie Taupin—beginning with the line, "Goodbye, England's Rose." However, even this moving performance gave no hint as to the range of emotions that would be evoked when Diana's brother spoke.

Paying memorable tribute to Diana as "a symbol of selfless humanity...a very British girl who transcended nationality," Earl Charles Spencer rebuked the press, who had turned his sister into "the most hunted person of the modern age." Vowing to protect his nephews from such treatment, he then isolated the royals by promising Diana "On behalf of your mother and sisters I pledge that we, your blood family, will do all we can to continue the imaginative and loving way in which you were steering these two exceptional young men, so that their souls are not simply immersed by duty and tradition, but can sing openly as you planned."

An extraordinary speech, unlike anything heard before at an event of this magnitude, it delivered a telling blow to Britain's staggering sovereignty. How the Earl would follow through on his challenge is yet to be seen, but from this day on, one thing was certain: The torch of hope lit by Princess Diana was now passing on to her eldest son, and it would be through the future King William V that the monarchy would have its greatest chance of survival.

Bibliography

[1] Moore, Sally. *The Definitive Diana—An A to Z Guide.* London: Sidgwick & Jackson, Ltd., 1991, and Coronet, 1992.

[2] Campbell, Lady Colin. *Diana in Private—The Princess Nobody Knew.* New York: St. Martin's Press, 1992.

[3] Morton, Andrew. *Diana: Her True Story.* New York: Simon & Schuster, 1992.

[4] Morrow, Ann. *Princess.* London: Chapmans Publishers, Ltd., 1991.

[5] Corby, Tom. *HRH The Princess of Wales—The Public Life.* London: Robert Hale, 1991.

[6] Morton, Andrew. *Diana's Diary—An Intimate Portrait of the Princess of Wales.* London: Michael O'Mara Books, Ltd., 1990.

[7] Holden, Anthony. *Charles: A Biography.* London: George Weidenfeld & Nicolson, Ltd., 1988.

[8] Cathcart, Helen. *Charles—Man of Destiny.* London: W.H. Allen, 1988.

[9] And assorted articles from the following publications through 1997: *People* Magazine, *Newsweek* Magazine, *Time* Magazine, *The Los Angeles Times,* and *The Washington Post.*

All quotes detailed in the present tense and without a reference are original.

Photo credits:

Front cover: **Snowdon/Camera Press/Globe Photos**

Back cover: **Alpha/Globe Photos**: Chambury, Dave Chancellor

AP/Wide World Photos; Alpha/Globe Photos: Dave Chancellor, Bryn Colton, Stewart Mark, Snowdon; **Archive Photos; Black Star:** Tom Sobolik, John Troha; **Corbis-Bettmann/Reuters/UPI; Gamma Liaison:** Butler/Spooner, Alex Tehrani; **Tim Graham/Sygma; G. Harvey/Stills/Retna; Edward Hirst/London Features International; Impact; Photoreporters, Inc.:** Picture Power, John Shelley; **Rex USA, Ltd.;** Cassidy & Leigh, Arthur Edwards/The Sun, James Gray, David Hartley, Nils Jorgensen; **Sipa-Press:** Aslan, Barthelemy, Dalmds, Fraser, Anwar Hussein, Special Features.